The
SPOILT
Generation

The
SPOILT
Generation

Why restoring authority
will make our children and
society happier

Dr Aric Sigman

piatkus

PIATKUS

First published in Great Britain in 2009 by Piatkus

Reprinted 2009 (twice)

A CIP catalogue record for this book
is available from the British Library

ISBN 978-0-7499-4148-2

Typeset in Sabon by M Rules
Printed and bound in Great Britain by
MPG Books, Bodmin, Cornwall

Papers used by Piatkus are natural, renewable and
recyclable products sourced from well-managed forests and certified in
accordance with the rules of the Forest Stewardship Council.

Mixed Sources
Product group from well-managed
forests and other controlled sources
www.fsc.org Cert no. SGS-COC-004081
© 1996 Forest Stewardship Council
FSC

Piatkus
An imprint of
Little, Brown Book Group
100 Victoria Embankment
London EC4Y 0DY

An Hachette UK Company
www.hachette.co.uk

www.piatkus.co.uk

Contents

Acknowledgements

I would like to thank my literary agent Sara Menguc for her encouragement and belief in the need for this book. Gill Bailey and Anne Lawrance, for originally seeing that there was a book to be written and a debate to be had. My editor, Anne Lawrance, who allowed me to write a book that trespassed beyond the boundary of parenting guide and whose objectivity and good judgement enabled me to finish it on time. Copyeditor Anne Newman, for demanding that what I wrote made sense. To my brother Karl, a dedicated father, with whom I had many very helpful discussions on the telephone during the writing of this book. To the many adults and children I've met abroad who've given me a unique perspective on this subject. And to my wife Katy, who encouraged me to put pen to paper on the subject she and I have spent so much time discussing . . . and then spending even more time discussing what I had actually put on that paper.

Introduction

Oscar Wilde once spouted: 'All charming people, I fancy, are spoiled. It is the secret of their attraction.' Yet were he alive today, we might find Wilde abandoning his masochistic interpretation of what constitutes 'charming attraction' in favour of more intolerant-sounding dinner-party classics such as, 'Love is a boy, by poets styled, Then spare the rod, and spoil the child'. He may even have been stirred to write a caustic parenting guide.

Today, there are deep problems in the socialisation of our children and young people, and our unease about exerting authority, along with our inability to distinguish between being authoritative versus authoritarian, is partly to blame. It's been far easier and more fashionable to be obsequious in the face of 'youth culture', and tolerance has been the zeitgeist. The lack of cultural and political will to acknowledge and address these problems has been cowardly and unprincipled. I'd say even more appalling than the spoilt children.

My views on this subject are the product of an unusual blend of my own experiences and professional background. I have four children, and because I'm self-employed I spend a lot of time with them (as well as with other people's children), giving me a day-to-day hands-on conception of parenting. I say this not with a sense of smug one-upmanship, but to make it clear that my understanding of children is more than academic. I also travel. My addiction to street anthropology has led me around the world to places such as North Korea, Bhutan, Mali, Tonga, Myanmar, Borneo, Laos, Iran, Vietnam, Bolivia, Burkina Faso, Far Eastern Siberia, Sumatra, South Korea and Cambodia, among others. Albeit informal, this approach to understanding children, parenting and society has been invaluable. I've seen universal patterns that have convinced me of some fundamental principles in child welfare and development that transcend time and space and are not subject to the whims of fashion.

I've spent today, for example, in Sarawak Borneo with a large group of seventeen-year-old conscripts in the Program Latihan Khidmat Negara (PLKN), the Malaysian national service. In addition to cultivating nation-building patriotism, the three-month spell is intended to instil a spirit of caring and volunteerism within society, to develop 'positive characteristics' among the young, with a heavy emphasis on community service and civic responsibility. My experience truly rubs in how the other half behaves. Hearing teenagers address me in terms of 'Excuse me, sir' seems as exotic as the knowledge that some of their recent ancestors were headhunters (I saw the shrunken heads hanging in their villages). These young people respect me just because I'm an adult and a human being, and none of it seems contrived. As I walk along the path, they naturally move aside to let me pass. They offer to shake my hand, smiling, as if they're genuinely pleased to see me.

My day-to-day anthropology back home is equally informative. I live in Brighton, Britain's San Francisco-cum-Amsterdam. The social terrain is a veritable Rift Valley of child evolution offering the observer every conceivable form of family structure and parenting style.

Finally, I've lived long enough to compare a golden age of easiness and indulgence with other times. Yet today, I find our children – 'freedom's orphans' – choking on our tolerance.

There are far-reaching consequences to the way we parent

and the kind of children we are now rearing. As I read the news headlines and the ongoing debates about the state we're in, the origins can, increasingly, be traced to the lack of authority children received from their parents and the adult figures in society who should also be socialising our children. By removing boundaries and retreating from authority, we adults have, it seems, failed our children, robbing them of their basic supporting structures.

Taking a variety of underlying issues by the scruff of the neck, this book will help, I hope, to halt our retreat from authoritative parenting, thereby reversing this modern-day form of abandonment.

The landscape of spoiling starts at home with parenting. Parents have a *duty* to try to bring up socially viable children. If we accept that we live in a society, then we must accept that child-rearing is not merely a question of personal style. We have an overriding responsibility not just to rear our children to our own satisfaction, but to the satisfaction of others as well. In most societies around the world, bad parenting that produces badly behaved children has a sense of stigma attached to it, along with accountability and shame, all of which act as a self-regulating mechanism for that society. So, why should we suspend judgement about ourselves when it comes to the most important role on earth?

But it isn't only parents who are crucial in socialising our children. Grandparents, teachers and policy-makers alike all need to be part of an honest and uncompromising reappraisal of how we can redress the status quo, redefine our roles and, together, create a more unified approach. In so doing, we will cultivate better-behaved and *happier* children, who, in turn, will cast off their reputation as the spoilt generation.

One

Little Emperors: Their Rise to the Throne
Children's growing sense of entitlement

Anyone over forty who claims that today's children are more spoilt than their predecessors will most likely be dismissed as being middle-aged and out of touch with the children of today. Historians are ushered in to remind us that, 'This is nothing new ... you really must read a bit more history, old chap.' We all feel more comfortable when we surrender to intellectual laziness and lean on well-worn refrains such as 'history repeats itself' and 'nothing is new'. The dismissive evidence is brought forward, the best examples being attributed controversially to figures ranging from Aristophanes, Socrates, Plato and Hesiod to Peter the Hermit – all of it a pot pourri of ancient disdain: 'The children now love luxury. They have bad manners, contempt for authority, they show disrespect to their elders ... They no longer rise when elders enter the room. They contradict their parents, chatter before company, gobble up dainties at the table, cross their legs, and are tyrants over their teachers.' (Fifth century BC (?)) Sound familiar? Read on ...

'The young people of today think of nothing but themselves. They have no reverence for parents or old age. They are impatient of all restraint. They talk as if they alone knew everything and what passes for wisdom with us is foolishness with them. As for girls, they are forward, immodest and unwomanly in speech, behaviour and dress.' And isn't it reassuring to know that the ancient philosophers were just as doom-laden as today's cultural commentators? 'Children are now tyrants, not the servants of their households.' And, 'I see no hope for the future of our people if they are dependent on frivolous youth of today, for certainly all youth are reckless beyond words . . . When I was young, we were taught to be discreet and respectful of elders, but the present youth are exceedingly wise [disrespectful] and impatient of restraint.' (Hesiod, eighth century BC (?))

It would be easy to end this discussion here because, of course, 'history repeats itself' and 'nothing is new', but I believe that our children are now making history and there is a new backdrop to the stage in this repeat performance.

By the way, successive spoilt generations can lead to entropy – the inevitable and steady deterioration of a system or society. Entire empires have crumbled because of spoiling.

The science of spoiling

The first things that come to mind when we think of a spoilt child are too many material goods and a physical appearance of chubby excess borne of laziness and too much choice and access to junk food. Of course, all of this is generally true about our children. They are, in terms of material goods and adipose tissue, richer and fatter than ever before, born during a bull market of often double-income parents with access to credit that their grandparents hadn't even heard of. If this is the case, then the credit crunch and economic recession should soon put paid to this latest historical outbreak of spoiling.

But many of us already know that this is only a small part of the picture. It is still quite possible for a child to be fat and rich, yet unspoilt. But it's even more possible for a child to be all three. And it can be done remotely and cross borders: the Philippine Institute for Development Studies reported in 2008 that Filipinos working abroad have spawned 'a generation of instant gratification and spoilt children'. Parents usually ply their kids with material luxuries, such as mobile phones, to make up for their absence in the family, then use their children's good academic performance as a measure of the positive effect of their migration. 'But deep inside, here is a person who is trying to look for a sense of self.'[1] Ironically, spoiling is often the result of *deprivation* – in particular, a parental attention deficit – and the materialism is a decoy that has duped us, frequently being used by less involved parents to mask this parental shortfall. It's also far easier to point to physical material goods and hard cash or even plastic as the spoils of spoiling because more abstract concepts, such as parent-to-child eye contact and attention, are harder to get our teeth into.

Unlike with fashionable subjects such as 'self-esteem', there's little empirical study or hard facts to shed light on what we mean by 'spoilt children'. This is partly due to the fact that the term has gone underground, much of what we used to call bad or spoilt behaviour having been sensitively rebranded as 'lacking adequate social skills'. I personally love the ring of this attempt at a definition of spoilt as a mindset: a spoilt child is a child with a sense of entitlement – 'I deserve whatever I want' – a child with less empathy and sympathy, more interested in himself than others.

I also see another dimension that amplifies this sense of entitlement: the increasing expectation of instant gratification. Another way of describing this is a reduction in our children's 'impulse control'. It isn't merely a case of a child wanting something; nowadays, they *expect* to get it, and more quickly than ever before. This could be explained as the result of the click-and-see and click-and-buy culture of screen technology, but this too has been amplified by big shifts in parenting, social values and legislation. Of course, every child is born selfish and the centre of their own universe, and whether that child is the son of Socrates or Paris Hilton or the daughter of Joe the plumber, we as parents have to shape and socialise the souls, values and actions of our noble savages, who may have no thought for the feelings of others and whose behaviour only serves their own needs and comforts. It is called civilising our children. But there have been unprecedented obstructions to our efforts.

From this unrefined mindset of entitlement, emotional disregard and weakened impulse control come many of the things that we complain about and that make up the facts and figures detailing society's ills. However, much of the landscape of spoilt behaviour is formed at a terribly subtle level. Nuances in body language, such as a lack of or delay in eye contact, disrespect in voice inflection, a pause in reaction, can all denote a profound change in recognition and respect. At a slightly more visible level, perhaps, is a lack of acknowledgement on the pavement, whereby children don't move aside or make way when an adult walks by. All too often now, it is the mountain that must move for the Little Emperor.

In discussing any sensitive subject nowadays, the intellectual coward always regurgitates the default mantra: the need for 'evidence-based conclusions'. Yet any true scientist realises that beyond the realpolitik of research grants and the 'publish or perish' confines of their intellectual ghetto lies the human condition, which is often difficult to measure and where we have to use good judgement to draw conclusions. There isn't a way in which to 'prove', definitively, that children and young people are more spoilt, but there is plenty of circumstantial evidence if you're set on the need for a so-called 'evidence-based' discussion.

We don't need no education

To start with, most teachers who have been in the job for several decades report that there have been significant changes for the worse in children's sense of entitlement and concern for – or even awareness of – others' feelings and in the behaviour that goes with this. For example, 'spoilt children' and the serious implications of them for schools and society was, for the first time, the main theme of the general secretary's speech at the Association of School and College Leaders annual conference in 2008. John Dunford saw parents as failing in their duty to instil basic moral values and acceptable conduct in their children, arguing that for too many children school was the only place where they experienced clear moral boundaries. In particular, Dunford said, inconsiderate attitude and bad manners have to be reversed, along with teaching children not to eat solely with their hands but how to use a knife and fork. Dunford concluded that it is, perhaps, a sad indictment on the present age that we accept the need to help parents to play their natural part and to rediscover what being a parent means.

'Teachers Under Pressure', a report published by Cambridge University's Faculty of Education in 2008, identified a growing trend of children at primary school who challenge teachers and throw tantrums in class. There was a general pattern of disobedience at home spilling into classrooms and the report cited 'highly permissive' parenting and misguided discipline policies in schools, resulting in poor pupil behaviour reaching the highest levels. Confrontational children were often found to be imitating their parents who often undermined teachers' authority by failing to support their disciplinary measures. 'Five years ago, primary teachers blamed the behaviour problems on an insufficiently motivating curriculum. Now teachers blame a rapidly changing social scene. By the time they come to school, many of these children have become expert in manipulating adults.' And for those who sleep easily, assuming that this applies only to the lower orders, the lead researcher pointed out, 'It does, to some extent, run across social class . . .'[2]

The difference between the son of Socrates and the child of today is that the old teacher–philosopher was complaining about miscreants who were *five times* the age of today's spoilt generation – teens and young men – while the reports quoted above refer to children as young as three. Low-level civil disobedience now has a youth market or, in fact, a toddler market. One graphic snapshot of this trend is the significant rise in rapes and sexual assaults actually taking place in London schools during 2008/9 reported by the Metropolitan Police. Their statistics suggest the vast majority of victims were school children under the age of sixteen and as many as one-in-three were under eleven.

This heralds a tipping point. From aristocracy to underclass, our children are now spoilt in ways that go far beyond materialism. We feel we've given them so much in terms of legislation, rights, opportunities and experiences. Indeed, on the surface, society has never done so much for its children. However, far from being protected, their wellbeing enhanced, our children are suffering in ways we could never have expected. And the consequences are measurable: we now have the highest rates of child depression, child-on-child murder, underage pregnancy, obesity, violent and anti-social behaviour and pre-teen alcoholism since records began. According to a study by UNICEF of twenty-one industrialised countries – 'An Overview of Child Well-being in Rich Countries' (2007) – there is no strong relationship between per capita GDP and child well-being. Even before the recession, when their economies were riding high, Britain and the US ranked bottom in most tables for child wellbeing. Britain's children are the unhappiest in the West, and are among the least satisfied with life, being described as a 'picture of neglect'.[3] Furthermore, a recent government-funded review highlighted research spanning twenty-five years and found that the prevalence of many mental health problems has doubled since the 1970s. One in ten children – that's more than a million – now has a clinically recognisable disorder such as depression, anxiety, anorexia or severe anti-social behaviour. And millions more may have 'lower-level' mental health problems that do not warrant a diagnosis, but cause concern and put them at risk of struggling at school. Interestingly, the report suggests that 'at least one good parent–child relationship' could help to reduce children's risk.[4]

These are the many cracks that have ultimately produced the Broken Britain endlessly discussed by political parties and the media, who themselves have blood on their hands and a smoking pistol in their studies. And the same general trends are emerging in all industrialised countries.

Death of the inner parent

Even as we chant 'put children first' ever louder, we have actually retreated from parenting. We used to parent far more. Yet in the space of a few decades, the way we parent has changed dramatically. Something we once did unknowingly and intuitively has been elevated to a fine science and become the subject of political fashion, the province of gurus, experts and TV nannies.

As parents, we are older and more time-poor than ever before, and we have the highest proportion of single-parent households in history. Our resourceful children have learnt successfully to manipulate their tired, overworked or separated parents to their own advantage, and are now spoilt in ways that extend beyond possessions and the confines of the family home. So we have to start asking direct questions: why has compulsion been replaced by the politically correct alternatives of persuasion and negotiation as the 'right' approach to shaping our children's behaviour? Is parental guilt behind the trend of parents saying 'No' with a sense of apology in their voice?

Spoilt behaviour is making a growing impression in every area of society, from the classroom and workplace, to the streets, criminal courts and rehab clinics.

Death of the outer parent

The erosion of our parental influence has also been caused by a variety of external measures ostensibly intended to protect our children, yet often merely disempowering us, their parents, and ultimately achieving the opposite. We need to ask ourselves further direct questions. For example, how and who has undermined the ability of parents, teachers, doctors and the police to help our children to become socially viable adults? And do laws that criminalise those of us who dare to smack our children erode our authority? A parent who holds their daughter by the wrists to prevent her from going out to have underage sex with a married man can be charged with assault. The Data Protection Act frequently prevents parents from discussing important things about their child's mental or physical health with the family GP. And the parental authority of separated fathers has been weakened by the Children Act, the Family Law Act and Child Support Agency at a time when children desperately need authoritative responsible fathers.

The act of parenting does not stop and start at our front door. In a civilised society, it extends into the wider community. At one time, there was an unspoken understanding that neighbours, teachers, policemen, even strangers were, in effect, deputised to deal with our children. However, there has been an almost complete reversal of this dynamic. Teachers are often challenged by parents when children are chastised, and a new study by the General Teaching Council has found that, ultimately, four in ten new teachers are driven out of the profession within two years,[5] while strangers may be either beaten up or arrested by the police for assault if they attempt to control unruly children, even when they are breaking criminal law.

If we are to dignify our living circumstances with the term 'society', we must now recreate a state of joined-up parenting in the fullest sense of the word, as this will make it easier on all of us, especially our children. And we need to begin by restoring authority to the adult figures in our children's world.

Two

Friend or Führer?
The role of authority

Adolf Hitler must bear some of the responsibility for spoiling our children. One of his many untried war crimes was to set in motion an aversion to authority that lingers today. Hitler gave authority a bad name.

Authority has been horribly misconstrued when it comes to dealing with our children. Sixty years after the Führer's demise, many of us who should be figures of authority – parents, teachers, policemen, doctors – have gone to great lengths to obscure obvious signs of hierarchy and control. Some liberal, middle-class parents even encourage their children not to call them Mummy and Daddy, but by their first names instead. And many parents, celebrities – even former members of the Royal Family – now causally refer to their children as their best friends. This loosening-up of overt hierarchy and power relations may seem cosy and kind, but it has helped to undermine our authority. Through a failure to distinguish between authoritarian and authoritative, best friend and superior, our parental roles have become less defined. We've done ourselves out of a job. There is a growing recognition that the tail is now wagging the dog, and this is not good for either.

As news of Nazi atrocities and genocide emerged from the Western Front in the 1940s, psychologists were desperate to understand and to prevent future generations of children from either idolising a fascist or from becoming one themselves. Halfway across the world, a team of researchers assembled at the University of California, announcing in 1950 that they had identified a personality type: 'the authoritarian personality' or 'TAP' for short. If a person was an authoritarian type, or a fascist in the making, this would be revealed in their psychometric profile on the diagnostic test, 'The F Scale' (F for fascist). With an F-score of between 3 and 4.5, they would be within normal limits and unlikely to be a Führer or Führerin in the making. Above this level, however, they'd be considered to be in possession of a 'pre-fascist' personality, possibly destined for a life of significant bossiness – or, in a worst-case scenario – a career of fascist dictatorship.

The part of this story that's relevant to parenting is the psychologists' belief that harsh and punitive parenting caused children to identify with and idolise authority figures, contributing to a 'pre-fascist' personality. The researchers published the classic book *The Authoritarian Personality* in 1950 which became highly influential, reverberating throughout many areas of thought, including child development and parenting.

No sooner had authority been brought into question as one fascist passed away, than the Cold War produced another demagogue: the 1950s right-wing, authoritarian, anti-Communist bully Joseph McCarthy. An unprecedented witch-hunt for Communist sympathisers or folk who just seemed downright 'un-American' made McCarthyism a byword for fearful conformity and obedience to authority and conservative American ideals. This would provide some of the baby-boom generation – and Bob Dylan – with something to rebel against . . . authority and the crew-cut that went with it. Many young people grew their hair long and protested against authority of all sorts, just because it was there. They then became parents and politicians.

And the story continues: in 1961, psychologist Stanley Milgram became curious about how a stout, little, testicularly challenged, dark-haired Austrian had managed to convince tall, blond German people that he should lead them to the ultimate supremacy they deserved and to go on and enlist a million people as 'accomplices in the Holocaust . . . were [they] just following orders? Could we call them all accomplices?' Milgram wondered.

Unlike his predecessors, who had focused more on identifying those who might become authoritarian demagogues, Milgram wanted to know what a figure of authority could persuade people to do on his behalf purely by virtue of his authority. Through a series of experiments conducted at Yale University, Milgram became the man who literally shocked the world. He exposed our willingness to obey an authority figure who instructs us to perform acts that utterly conflict with our personal conscience, by giving innocent people fatal 450-volt electric shocks. Milgram's subjects believed they were part of an experiment supposedly dealing with the relationship between punishment and learning. The figure of respectable authority (the experimenter) – a stern, impassive biology teacher dressed in a grey technician's coat – instructed participants to deliver an electric shock to a learner by pressing a lever on a machine each time the learner made a mistake on a word-matching task. The intensity of the shock would increase by 15-volt increments with each learner error, starting at 15 volts for the first and peaking at an 'extreme-intensity' final solution at 450 volts for the very final error.

In reality, the shock device was a prop (complete with electric shock sound effects for different voltages) and the learner was an actor who did not actually get shocked, but conjured up authentic screams of agony. As the voltage of the shocks climbed, the

actor started to bang on the wall that separated him from his tor-
mentor. After banging on the wall several times and complaining
about his heart condition, his responses would finally stop and it
would go silent. Despite the obvious agony of the victim, however, the majority of the subjects (two-thirds) continued to obey
to the end, believing they were delivering 450-volt shocks, simply
because the experimenter commanded them to. In fact, only one
person refused to continue the shocks *before* reaching 300 volts.

This classic experiment on authority has been repeated in different settings and different countries, but our response to
authority remains disturbingly high. In fact, in 2009 the
American Psychological Association announced the results of a
new study: 'Nearly fifty years after one of the most controversial
behavioural experiments in history . . . people are still just as
willing to administer what they believe are painful electric
shocks to others when urged on by an authority figure.
Obedience rates [are] essentially unchanged.'[1] The percentage of
people prepared to inflict fatal electric shocks remains remark-
ably constant at 61–66 per cent, regardless of time or place – a
finding that should please multiculturalists.

Milgram's home truth about authority and the 'free will' of
the people hit a nerve. The *New York Times* was aghast: 'Sixty-
five per cent in test blindly obey order to inflict pain.' Later,
Milgram was denied tenure at Harvard after becoming an assistant professor there. The truth was too dangerous . . . and
politically incorrect.

Milgram's influential 1974 book, *Obedience to Authority:
An Experimental View* was accompanied by his influential
magazine article, 'The Perils of Obedience', in which he
lamented the dire consequences of authority:

> Stark authority was pitted against the subjects' [participants']
> strongest moral imperatives against hurting others and, with
> the subjects' ears ringing with the screams of the victims,

authority won more often than not. The extreme willingness
of adults to go to almost any lengths on the command of an
authority constitutes the chief finding of the study and the fact
most urgently demanding explanation.

Ordinary people simply doing their jobs and without any
particular hostility on their part can become agents in a terrible destructive process. Moreover, even when the destructive
effects of their work become patently clear, and they are asked
to carry out actions incompatible with fundamental standards
of morality, relatively few people have the resources needed to
resist authority.[2]

Class-ridden authority

Britain continues to have her own axe to grind with authority:
her class system.

The growing erosion of authority is, partly, a long-awaited
reaction to the Victorian era of which Thomas Carlyle
(1795–1881) said: 'The time for levity, insincerity, and idle babble
and play-acting, in all kinds, is gone by; it is a serious, grave
time.' The social constraints of Victorianism were followed by the
Defence of the Realm Act (DORA), passed during the early
weeks of the First World War, giving the government wide-
ranging powers, such as censorship (and you weren't allowed to
fly a kite, light a bonfire or feed wild animals bread, for that
matter). DORA ushered in a variety of authoritarian social-
control mechanisms. And, later, the Second World War was
accompanied by propaganda posters proclaiming, 'Be Like Dad,
Keep Mum' or '[keep your mouth shut] You Never Know Who's
Listening!' and rationing books. My mother-in-law tells me how
excited she was finally to gossip and see a banana again in 1950.

Authority continued to prevail, and children did as they were
told '. . . because I said so'. Many of my British friends of a certain age tell me: 'It's all right for you with your beach-boy

upbringing, but you really have no idea what it was like over here until recently: the conformity, the emotional repression. You were a citizen, we were Her Majesty's subjects; and while you had doughnuts, we had duties; you had a life, we had a *station* in life.' Coming from a culture in which self-adoring loudmouths and show-offs are commonplace, this social and emotional history is still a revelation to me.

British public school reinforced an obedience to authority through the cane, birch or, for the more fortunate, the slipper. And there was the character-building backdrop of cold showers and the humbling lavvy cubicles with no doors. In some schools, each pupil had to note down and sign confirmation of their morning bowel movement, as they were expected to regularise their bodily functions to conform with the expectations of their housemaster. But many parents and those in positions of authority and influence today have mixed feelings about that long walk to Headmaster's office, not to mention the fagging system. It's not surprising they've been left with a jaded view of authority, and, for some, an inclination to be trussed up and disciplined.

In the recent push for a more 'classless' society, authority has understandably become a casualty. The British feel enigmatically ambivalent towards their class system. Like a well-worn security blanket, it is familiar and has defined everything from their historical influence in the world to their divinely sour comedy. Yet at the same time, they feel the blanket needs to be replaced or torn apart: the class system is unfair, in some way unnatural and certainly wrong.

Various forms of privilege, hierarchy and disparity, including inequality in social status, power, opportunity or money, are the obvious targets in striving for a classless society. Disparity is a reminder of unjust privilege, and so its erosion has been seen as a sensible aim . . . up to a point.

Hierarchies of standards in areas of culture and education are tainted with notions of elitism. Excellence, it is feared, excludes.

So the solution is to diminish the hierarchy by lowering such standards and dumbing down. A hierarchy of spoken English, where to be well spoken is considered better than not being well spoken, is resolved through the growing use of Estuary English by many middle-class people – and BBC presenters. A hierarchy of morality, where certain behaviours are deemed explicitly better than others, is softened through moral relativism.

And, of course, hierarchies and disparities in authority have been an obvious bugbear to the architects of the classless society. As soon as you open a dictionary or thesaurus, it becomes clear that the whole concept of authority is in need of a public relations firm. The synonyms for authority run from bad to worse (command, control, domination, force, might, power, sovereignty, supremacy, sway), while the definition of authority – 'the power to command, control or judge others' – doesn't have much of a New Age ring to it either. And its close relative authoritarian, defined as 'considering obedience to authority more important than personal freedom', rings alarm bells.

After all, if you're in favour of a classless society, authority is in rather an uncomfortable position because it smacks of something you submit to and submission sounds similar to subjugation, which could lead to a servant/master relationship, and before you know it, one's upstairs and the other one's downstairs. A populist mindset of 'people shouldn't feel more important and lord it over other people . . . we should be a more equal society' may seem fine, when you're talking about civil rights. But Britain's class revision has also taken some of the hierarchy out of parenting and made it more of a consensual affair among equals.

The authority channel

Our authority-shy misadventure has been further exacerbated by our complicity in elevating youth culture to the highest altar. Age now confers little seniority and the natural democratic hierarchy that has served societies and generations has suddenly been inversed. This is the most striking difference between our culture and that of the remote places I visit. I remember seeing a documentary several years ago in which the presenter was the first white man in living memory to visit the Adi people in the Arunachal Pradesh region of India. He interviewed an Adi elder who also acted as the tribal medicine woman. Two sentences in particular stood out for me. When asked about her, presumably, high matriarchal status, the woman pointed out forlornly: 'The young people go to the other villages and see television. Now they don't respect me any more.'

If you can be bothered to examine many of the mainstream soaps, sitcoms and dramas you'll soon find that when middle-aged and older people appear on television, they often seem to have 'earned' their place only because they can emulate the behaviours of younger people. Increasingly, I see older people on screen trying to ape the young: it's never hip, but always promises to be simply undignified. And the same is happening with our political leaders: the former US secretary of state and army general Colin Powell recently performed a hip-hop dance routine alongside well-known rap artists, complete with embarrassing hand movements.

Connecting with young people does not mean imitating them and relinquishing your stature and seniority in the process. But one big obstacle to retaining our standing is a generation of parents who are determined not to appear uncool, sharing similar tastes in pop music with their children, whom they treat as their best 'mates'. The latest example I've seen in my town is the promotion in shop windows and kindergarten hallways of 'Baby Boogie – fun and funky afternoon clubbing for parents and children up to seven' held at a cocktail bar and 'featuring the very best soul & disco . . .'

So, in addition to seeking the approval of children, parents and figures of authority are increasingly befriending them – hardly a good basis for establishing respect and authority.

As I finished writing the last paragraph, my wife handed me an article by the editor of *Vogue*, entitled, 'Help! I'm a Slave to My Son'. It describes: 'a pathetic tendency to bathe in pleasure if I managed to elicit filial approval for any activity other than the handing out of cash . . . I notice, to my horror, that it is me who is desperately trying to conjure up teenage praise. I glow with inner pleasure if he likes some recherché tune I've downloaded on to my iPod . . . If we were sensible, we would all . . . allow ourselves to be viewed as "sad" oldies.'[3]

When older people appear in mainstream programmes, they are parodied as figures of fun. And the power relationship between older and younger people in both drama and factual programming forms another highly insidious part of television's new devotional position towards youth culture. In contemporary drama, older characters are spoken to as equals and, at times, subordinates by the more knowing younger characters. And when children's characters speak, it has been the fashion for them to hold court while parents take note or even obey the child's edicts. This affects the way young people treat older people in real life. Is it, therefore, surprising that older, or even middle-aged, people today are generally not appreciated as experienced elders or possessors of wisdom?

In many countries, the birth rate is falling and society is greying, yet the silver-haired sage is obsolescent on the screen. Instead, we are encouraged to revere the ideas and importance of the young as never before. The growing lack of respect for older people, reinforced and driven by the media, has eroded the social value of more than half of the population. Furthermore, it has weakened a long-established foundation of a civilised society. The effects on family and classroom discipline, and law and order are becoming clearer by the month. With youth culture, everyone is equal, so the older person has to earn respect. In other cultures I've visited, he is afforded respect naturally.

Our veneration of youth culture is also betraying and damaging our children. Young people crave and need figures of authority, if only as a frame of reference to rebel against. This is a necessary part of their development. But when their elders end up trying to emulate them, it's actually unsettling and confusing for them and the rest of society. After all, someone has to be older and unfunky on television and in real life to enable the young to feel . . . well, young. And in a world that changes more quickly in every other aspect, older people serve as a form of continuity and quiet reassurance. Given the detrimental effects of high rates of divorce and our increasingly mobile society, this is particularly so for children. To deprive the young of these things is selfish and short-sighted.

When I was in China, I was told they would be celebrating the Year of the Old Person, something I couldn't imagine ever happening in Britain. Historically, Chinese society has placed their elderly on a pedestal. Respect for older people was an integral part of Confucian doctrine, especially for the family patriarch.

And I have found the same invisible hierarchy appearing in completely different cultures I've visited, such as in Iran, South Korea and in the villages of Mali and Burkina Faso. Travelling on a tiny motorcycle, covered with red clay dust from the paths, to somewhere west of Bobo-Dioulasso and south of Ougadougou, I passed a scene like something out of *National Geographic* and another era: a casual, yet neat, line of women walking for miles with enormous containers and sacks on their heads, often with no hands needed to balance their burdens. In this line, the older women (perhaps in their late twenties or early thirties) exuded a subtle, yet obvious, seniority over their juniors – an unspoken pecking order. When I arrived at my destination, a small village of mud-and-thatch hut-cum-cabins, I was led to the chief, who took pity on me in the searing heat and asked someone to give me a drink of what I think was sugar palm juice. He explained that he was the head of the council of elders, who made decisions for the village because they were older, more experienced and wiser. Unfortunately, his think-tank seemed to be taking a siesta, so I didn't get to see them in session.

In other countries, some tribes eat their elders (after they die naturally) to gain wisdom. The Wari tribe in Brazil and the Fore tribe in New Guinea are thought to have practised funerary cannibalism. In most cultures, until recently, the wisdom of elders hasn't been something that requires any conscious recognition; older people are naturally respected and carry an inherent authority.

When greater authority, seniority and privilege are conferred incrementally with the accumulation of years, everyone feels they have an opportunity to gain increasing respect and influence as they grow older. This system also provides good social medicine – a second form of government, which has a most powerfully civilising effect. But as a result of globalised youth television dismantling this hierarchy of ageing, more countries are beginning to experience the social consequences.[4]

Every time I hear yet another ingratiating politician or radio or television interviewer gushing the stock phrase, 'Children today don't have a voice', I want to schedule a hearing test for them. Bumper-sticker-level slogans such as, 'We need to listen to young people', are like Chinese whispers, often interpreted as, 'We need to respond to what young people say and want', and often taken as, 'We should do what young people want'. But this is a far cry from being aware of children and young people's needs, and acting as responsible figures of authority in deciding what is legitimate and in their best interests as their arbitrator and, ultimately, their superior. For those who are hard of hearing: children have had a loud voice for a long time, but that voice is often telling us what to do and in an irreverent tone. Our children's voice is not the only one we can listen to: there is always another dialogue whose message is at odds with the words being uttered. Like adults, children often don't actually know or cannot articulate what they want or need or mean; in fact, what a child says can literally obfuscate what may really be on their mind. Ignoring what someone says in favour of listening with our third ear – our intuition – and using our considered judgement and experience often enables us to hear more clearly.

Institutional disrespect

There is growing list of compelling reasons to unashamedly re-instate adult authority and hierarchy as an absolute necessity in relating to our children. A five-year government-funded study of 11,000 children has found they have less respect for authority figures and 'considerably' less for the police: children 'have declining levels of trust in authority figures and institutions, including family and teachers'.[5] And they're not hiding their feelings: the number of children, including ten-year-olds, convicting for violently attacking police officers has risen by at least 44 per cent in five years.

Erosion of authority is cascading across our society. You could call it institutionalised disrespect. Here are some of my own everyday highlights:

My wife and I recently took our seven-year-old son for an appointment with the consultant paediatric surgeon at our marvellous brand-spanking-new local children's hospital. The staff there bend over backwards to make children feel safe and comfortable. In fact, we've been told that when it's time for surgery, our son can drive his own little electric car to the anaesthetic room to be knocked out. The hospital authorities are clearly willing to go all out for the young: there is a games room for adolescents and teenagers with a sign on the wall warning that 'parents of patients and medical staff must ask [the adolescents'] permission to enter this room'.

When the time came for us to see the surgeon, our son was given a highly democratic questionnaire, asking him directly how he would like to address the senior surgeon: as Dr Bloggs, Mr Bloggs or just plain Fred. And there was a reciprocal deal on offer: 'How would you like the doctor to address you?' Like most children, my son was perplexed by the tyranny of options before him, wondering why an important medicine man couldn't simply treat him like a seven-year-old child with a first name and why he, as a seven-year-old, couldn't call the great medicine man Dr Bloggs or Professor Bloggs – or let his parents play a role in the proceedings and speak on his behalf at times.

At a time when violent assaults on hospital medical staff have reached an all-time high, there are signs up asking young people not to attack staff, otherwise 'we'll support the nurse in taking action against you if they choose to'. I was shocked and angered at the need for this sign in an intensive care unit for premature infants in incubators.

Another 'Please, would you mind . . .?' approach to exerting authority over children and the young popped up at my local supermarket checkout counter, where an apologetic sign for teenagers reads: 'Please don't be offended if we ask for proof of age when you buy alcohol.'

But my favourite example of 'Would you mind awfully . . .?' comes from a leaflet for Her Majesty's Court Service: 'To maintain a safe and secure environment, we would be grateful if you would not bring your knife into court in future.'[6]

These are the signs that the authorities have little authority.

In a pattern that is being played out across the industrialised world, a growing number of even very young children are now being disrespectful and violent towards teachers and nursery school staff. In Belgian schools, an increase in discipline problems among pupils has been noted in recent years. In 2008 it was reported that the number of children being excluded from schools there had almost doubled in five years, while in the same year, several thousand children in England and Wales aged between two and five were expelled or suspended from school for violent attacks against teachers and other children. Even the youngest children are throwing chairs, swearing and refusing to obey their teachers. Persistent disruption and uncontrollable behaviour is found to start at a younger age. Teaching organisations are now raising their heads above the parapet and complaining that 'permissive' parents are simply not displaying authority so their children can learn to respect it in the classroom and elsewhere.

Governments share a large part of the responsibility for this trend. The authority of our teachers has been systematically eroded over a period of time. Their power to stop bad behaviour in its tracks before it escalates into violence, and to deal with disruptive and violent children to maintain order in the classroom, has been increasingly restricted. Ironically, even their ability to be kind and comforting to small children has been curtailed by fear of the potential consequences. This is described beautifully by the Council for Exceptional Children (CEC), the largest international body promoting special education. In their 1997 article 'To Hug or Not to Hug?', still carried on their website today, they put it baldly: 'The question of whether or not to hug or touch a child is not an easy one . . . Is giving a child a hug worth the risk of being sued and losing your career?'[7]

And as our children become ever more aware of their teacher's limitations in sanctioning or even being kind to them, their teachers are busy telling them about their rights as part of the curriculum. In fact, as 'an excellent starting point for global citizenship', UNICEF published a manifesto in 2008 for schools[8] entitled, 'Teaching about children's rights':

- Children and young people have rights
- Children and young people should be informed about their rights
- Children and young people should be helped to exercise their rights

- Children and young people should be able to enforce their rights
- There should be a community of interest to advocate young people's rights

Interestingly, a parliamentary working group convened by ministers and the Department for Children, Schools and Families in 2009 uncovered a sharp rise in allegations made by pupils against teachers. Yet, the vast majority of these allegations were found to be false or malicious, with only 2 per cent resulting in cautions or convictions. The general secretary of the NASUWT union pointed to an unhealthy shift in power and authority: 'In some cases, pupils know their rights and not their responsibilities. We have had cases where pupils have been quite open in saying that if they make an allegation against a teacher they know it will get them into serious trouble.'

When I recently did some voluntary teaching in Cambodia, the only disruption in the classroom was that of the young pupils scrambling to get hold of the pencils and paper I had supplied so they could exercise their 'right' to write. Authority in school is not the privilege of the rich industrialised world. These children were barefoot and many had no electricity in their floating houseboats, but their eyes were glowing with warmth and enthusiasm at being in class and able to learn.

Policing has also relinquished authority. You might have noticed that the term police 'service' is replacing police 'force'. I've become more and more aware of a change in respect for the police's authority when I see the way people behave towards authority in other countries I visit.

In Khabarovsk, in far eastern Siberia, society and authority are in flux and I had a glimpse of the successor to hard-line Communism. A local mother told me: 'Yes, there have been big changes – but not for the better. People think they can do whatever they want . . . and so they do. It's called democracy. Before perestroika and the liberalising of our government's authority, people were politer, more respectful and genuinely nicer to one another. We were happier. Then rudeness, disrespect and self-ishness started.'

A while back, I was at a restaurant in Bukkitingi, West Sumatra, when a police sergeant came up to me and introduced himself. He spoke excellent English and was interested in England and America. His colleagues soon joined us, and as I began to sketch for them a picture of their English counterparts, a look of incredulity replaced their warm Sumatran smiles. I told them of the stab-proof vests and lack of respect or fear that English crim-inals have for our men in blue and he, in turn, explained: 'I don't need a gun or stab-proof vest. I want to be personable, for people here to both like me and respect me. They address me as Pa.'

We continued chatting and I explained how in Britain and other European countries such as France and Spain, children who break the law are often approached by an awfully approachable Police Community Support Officer (PCSO). Their eyes widened further. The language just seems all wrong: servile and egalitarian. Children dub them the 'plastic police' because they have few powers – they can't disperse troublemakers or even detain suspects. But in 2008, grieving relatives attending a knife-crime summit near London didn't mince their words: 'Nobody ever thought it would come to this: ten-year-olds car-rying knives . . . All we ever see is those plastic police, the Police Community Support Officers, and the kids laugh at them because they know they're powerless to do anything.'[9]

I too have been a victim of overly polite and sensitive policing. It happened late at night on a narrow, dark street as I was walk-ing back to my bed and breakfast in St Ives in Cornwall. A car approached and pulled up on the pavement, shining its lights at me. I could only see the silhouette of a policewoman getting out of her patrol car. As she walked towards me, I instinctively put my hands up – the survival reflex of an American who is familiar with armed police accustomed to being shot at in the middle of the night by the suspects they stop to question. 'Excuse me, sir,' she said. 'Where have you just come from?' I explained that I was just a tourist 'staying in the bed and breakfast just over there . . . you can frisk me if you like'. She said, 'No, sir, there's no need for that,' and, after asking a few more rudimentary questions, she told me: 'It's just that someone in the vicinity, of your general description – a male with dark hair and dark blue coat – has committed a vehicle crime [breaking into a car] and we're look-ing for him.' I assured her, and she obviously believed me, that I wasn't her man. But what surprised me most was what immedi-ately followed my interrogation. She politely enquired, 'Sir, would you mind helping me fill out this form?' and held out a long, narrow yellow sheet headed, 'Explaining Police Powers to Stop and Search You . . . Know Your Rights!' It said: 'The police can speak to you during the course of their duties . . . They cannot detain you just because you are young . . .'

The questioning then began in earnest, covering name, address, height, sex, clothing removed: Yes/No. She then asked me: 'Which ethnic group would you say you belong to?' There were seventeen choices. She came across as politely as a cus-tomer service rep, saying, 'We value your arrest. Your stop and search is important to us.' It was, in effect, 'How was it for you?' However, I always felt that the way she treated me was somehow at odds with her name: Police Sergeant Bulley.

My interrogator's authoritarian-lite methods are now being reinforced by the Children's Commissioner for England. In the face of the tripling of murder rates of children by other children in the last three years, the Commissioner is concerned that stop-and-search powers being belatedly used by the police to curb such attacks might further antagonise young people: 'Anything that perpetuates the view that children are the troublemakers is a dangerous development.'

So those who do wrong are not the young people who commit most of the violent crime, but the adults who try to control them – which the Commissioner sees as 'demonising' them. He would like to have parents who smack their children prosecuted as criminals, believes that Britain has moved on from an age of authoritarianism when you did what you were told and has urged the police to 'understand' young people better. In reinforcing the view that children should *not* have to do what they are told, and, consequently, undermining our influence as parents, this reflects a view that has done significant harm to young people's development for the past four decades: that children should tell adults what to do.[10] This trend to befriend is highly irresponsible and reflects the selfish inclination of our leaders' desire to win favour with children, rather than protect them at the cost of their own popularity.

Pulling rank

By shying away from being in control and maintaining a clear position of authority, we have engaged in a type of parental and societal self-harm. Children today urgently need the most secure support network possible, in the form of boundaries, discipline and order, to keep them from crumbling. Yet instead, the adult world at every turn – from parents and teachers, to social workers, police, the courts and politicians – has retreated from authority, and in so doing has robbed children of their basic supporting structures. In a misguided attempt to appear more sensitive to children's needs, our institutions have shed much of their authority in favour of being accessible and less intimidating.

Children need teachers, school heads and other authority figures to provide order in their world. However, many children feel insecure going to school today. Bullies and weapon-toting kids seem to fear no one and a generalised lack of respect for authority permeates many schools.

As parents, we are confused: unable to confidently distinguish between being authoritative and authoritarian, many of us have chosen what appears to be the safer option. There seems to be an unconscious misperception that authority and sensitivity, love and compassion are in some way mutually exclusive, and that by exerting authority (including compulsion and threats) we, in some way, diminish the caring we want our children to have and the love and trust we want to feel from them.

In 2009, Britain's Institute of Education published a study involving 12,500 families and children, combined with a major research review, which concluded: 'Multiple studies have documented that children who have authoritative parents – that is, both firm disciplinarians and warm, receptive caregivers – are more competent than their peers at different developmental periods including preschool, school age and adolescence.' These conclusions will be unwelcome news for a generation of parents seduced by the culturally convenient, ingratiating parenting books that promote the idea of children merely needing a 'good enough parent'; 'the notion of "good enough" parenting may seem ideal in today's hectic world, yet the reality is that "good enough" parents will most likely produce "good enough" children at best. Girls appear to be particularly vulnerable to the risks of "good enough" parenting for behavioural and emotional outcomes. . . contrary to popular understanding, "better" or "authoritative" parenting characterised by high levels of maturity expectation, supervision, disciplinary efforts, sensitivity to and support for a child's needs leads to better-adjusted, more competent children.'[11]

Those who require more research in order to feel less queasy about exerting authority over our children may be interested to hear that between 2005 and 2009, cross-cultural studies with titles such as, 'Rules, legitimacy of parental authority, and obligation to obey in Chile, the Philippines, and the United States' have found strong links between a child's belief in rules and the validity of their parents' control and authority over them, as well as fewer behavioural problems and higher 'self-efficacy'. This trust in and acceptance of parental rules, control and authority is also 'an important predictor of the extent to which they are willing to obey parents and to disclose to them ... important in maintaining positive, respectful and trusting relations during adolescents' transition to autonomy'.[12]

So restoring authority does not, as some people might think, translate into being less kind, sensitive and loving towards our children. I would argue that pulling rank over our children is often a greater act of selflessness than being less judgemental and dominant. Parenting without boundaries might make us feel as if we are being 'nice', but while at first our children may enjoy getting away with things, they will eventually feel that their parents don't actually care enough to do the hard work of parenting. A child who feels his parents don't care about him will feel unsupported and is likely to experience more problems.

Let's be friends

It's a fact that some members of the current generation of parents have difficulty in setting and enforcing limits and boundaries for their children, unconsciously deciding that being their friend is more important than being their parent. But stop and think: friends are equals. Friends are at liberty to tell one another what they think and feel, to be confidantes. Childhood friends often impulsively, sometimes permanently, reject one another, moving on to other friendships as they continue learning about the wide variety of characters that life has to offer. A friend doesn't guide, nurture and protect, or set boundaries and limits with discipline in the way that a parent does.

When parents try to be friends with their children, it sends a confusing message. When our children break our rules, we'll need to enforce the right behaviour, but our children won't understand the change of role. This conflict of interest creates inconsistency in our role as parents and undermines our children's feelings of security.

Being a friend to our children is one way to sidestep the conflict, responsibility and pain of being a parent. It's also a good place to hide if we don't know *how* to parent. However, our role in our children's life is to be their parent, not their friend. This need not be an adversarial relationship, but simply one in which we make it clear who is in charge. This gives our children a solid, secure base from which they can explore the world. Friendship is conditional and does not provide this.

Despite what they say or do, our children realise underneath it all that they are, in fact, children, and don't know how to 'do' life yet. They do not really want to be in charge. If they feel that no one is in command and behaving like a parent, they'll often challenge our (lack of) authority, trying to provoke us into rising to the occasion. Obviously, in order to create a healthy relationship, we must be loving and just authoritative figures, but children want and need parents who are in control.

Not having a parent is the most fundamentally insecure feeling a child can have. If we don't know how to manage things, who does? This is an even more salient question today when a child's outer pillars, those of our schools and communities, have shed their authority – or had it stolen from them while they were asleep.

As children feel their way from the security of their home to negotiating the outside world, they continue to need handrails on their route to establishing independence and to becoming socially viable. It is our responsibility – as parents, grandparents, teachers, politicians, even strangers – to construct this supervised route to adulthood by ensuring that it is manned by figures who our children *know* are vested with authority. Anything less is self-indulgence, with the effect of spoiling our children.

Three

Crime and Punishment

Boundaries, rules . . . and consequences

I've yet to come across a parent, or even a childless hermit, who doesn't agree that children need boundaries and limits. However, there seems to be an enormous gap between our belief in the idea of these boundaries and actually constructing them. And a further gap appears when it comes to policing them. Yet the importance of drawing a line in the sand and reinforcing all those supposedly negative things – restrictions, boundaries, rules, punishments, power over a child – cannot be overstated.

I once had a brief glimpse of the abyss into which a few unfortunate parents stare every day. I was at my desk when the telephone rang. My wife was on the line, telling me that my thirty-three-month-old son had been hit by a car. Shocked, I asked if he was all right. 'I don't know,' she said. 'The ambulance has taken him to A&E, but he was crying and moving around when they picked him up and put him on the stretcher.' I immediately rang for a cab to take me to the hospital, and sat through what seemed like an endless journey with a growing sense of foreboding. When I arrived, I ran into the emergency room to see my son lying unconscious on the table in the middle of the room, with those harsh, clinical lights shining down on his peaceful face. I noticed a prominent bump on his forehead.

He had run into the road and was hit by a car travelling at about twenty-five miles per hour, yet he had bounced in an unusual way and escaped with a concussion. He was exceedingly lucky. My wife and I, on the other hand, were traumatised, haunted by what might have been.

I had gone to painstaking lengths to drill into all of our children that they must 'Stay out of the road', yet still this had happened. However, after the accident, I was sure that the unbeatable combination of being hit by a car and me reminding my son regularly of the experience and how it relates to running into the road would put him permanently off the idea. No such luck. No sooner had he recovered than he saw something across the road that interested him and ran towards it as I shouted to him to stop. I ran after him, grabbed him and gave him a whack on his backside, accompanied by a good shaking and topped with a generous burst of menacing shouting. But I don't find this amusing. And neither does a growing number of governments . . . for very different reasons. Twenty-three countries (eighteen of them European) now consider that what I did to my son constitutes a criminal offence. They have banned corporal punishment completely. And 106 countries have put a stop to corporal punishment in schools – including many where it was common only a generation ago.

New Zealand became the first English-speaking country to ban smacking. And there's been an attempt by a Californian politician to outlaw spanking of children under three. Violators could face up to a year in jail or a thousand-dollar fine. In some countries, parents and teachers are steadily losing the right to discipline children through the use of any force. And regardless of the law, social changes seem to be making parents cautious about smacking. Public campaigns on child abuse and popular parenting books on so-called positive discipline have even led many people who oppose a ban on corporal punishment to say, at least publicly, that they don't really consider the practice acceptable. When the subject comes up, I increasingly notice non-committal middle-class parents smiling nervously, others piously, making smug statements such as, 'We don't do violence in our house.'

Many non-spankers see spanking as a form of violence, and feel that a light parental cuff and serious violent beatings are points on the same spectrum, albeit quite far apart. They worry that most child abuse begins as a disciplinary swat that gets out of hand. This, to me, is like saying that domestic child sexual abuse starts with a father putting his daughter to bed and kissing her goodnight. Therefore, if we prevent fathers from tucking their daughters in bed at night and giving them a kiss, we could reduce the opportunity and therefore the incidence of fathers sexually abusing their daughters. Such a move would outrage my own daughters, and I'd like to think they'd bite and scratch the politician trying to 'protect' them.

A similar mindset increasingly bedevils many innocent aspects of family life. One of my young sons was recently in a county drama competition involving twelve schools. On the big night, the announcer informed parents that we shouldn't take any photographs of our own children on stage. The logic nowadays is that because paedophiles may get hold of and enjoy photographs of children and post them on the Internet, we should be deprived of enjoying the memory of our child's performance.

In opposing our right to discipline our own children physically, the California State Assembly Speaker Sally Lieber told the press in 2007: 'California's parents might need to give up that privilege for the sake of those who might use it repeatedly each day.' A case of perverse minoritarianism, where the distorted perceptions of the few are imposed on the many.

Beyond the arguments surrounding spanking children lies the

most worrying implication of all: a clear message that we parents cannot be trusted to love our own children; that we are unable to distinguish intuitively between a spank – in much the same way as a bear cuffs her cub – and a punch or a beating. This very modern position ignores and defies the very essence of what being a parent is. Publicly redefining and limiting parents so clinically in matters that are for most of the world, and have been for most of our history, intimate, intuitive and private, has served to undermine our authority and status as parents. For a child who witnesses an outside body coming into their home and disempowering their parent, their family structure is weakened by a shift in the balance of power. Such caring legislation has paradoxically helped to deprive children further of strong authority figures and the protection and reinforcement of boundaries that they badly need.

The nationalising, in effect, of this aspect of parenting at a point in history when parents need to regain authority and their children need boundaries that mean something, is the reason why the phrase 'the nanny state' was coined.

The rights stuff

Given the popularity of hijacking the concept of children's rights, I suggest a basic list we can work from:

- In a world and society that is changing more quickly and seems less stable and reliable, children have a right to the strongest possible supporting structures of boundaries, discipline and order to keep them from falling to pieces.
- Children have the right to expect the adult world – from parents to teachers, social workers, police, the courts and politicians – not to erode, but to reinforce these supports and not to blatantly retreat from authority . . . if only to provide the child with something solid to rebel against.

- Children have the right to have their behaviour and development shaped so they can become socially and emotionally viable adults. A child has the right to know that his parents love him enough to become sufficiently roused to confront and, if necessary, punish him, as opposed to overlooking his unacceptable behaviour or appeasing him for the sake of an easy life.
- A child has the right to a parent who will slap him on the wrist to teach him a life-saving lesson, as opposed to one who refuses to because they are either ideologically wed to a position or scared of what others might think.

Yet, instead, there seems to be a complete inversion of what should constitute our children's 'rights'. The UN Convention on the Rights of the Child declares: 'The right of the child to protection from corporal punishment and other cruel or degrading forms of punishment . . . asserting children's right to protection from all forms of violence . . . to prohibit all currently legalised violence against children . . . "physical" punishment as any punishment in which physical force is used and intended to cause some degree of pain or discomfort, however light. Most involves hitting ("smacking", "slapping", "spanking") children, with the hand. But it can also involve, for example . . . shaking.' And to think they want me in handcuffs.[1]

Many academics have joined the chorus of disapproval for slapping our children on the wrist. For example, Patricia L. Kaminski of the psychology faculty of the University of North Texas says, 'It's strange that in some things we are so far behind the world in human rights. We need to keep fighting on this front for children's rights.'

I can only imagine that many others so highly motivated to campaign for anti-spanking laws are fetishising a completely unremarkable aspect to ordinary parenting and using this issue as a conduit to chase their own childhood ghosts away. As is the case with much who-cares-wins legislation, making the transition from social engineering to criminal law, an emotionally driven minority group simply cares a lot more than the rest of us about an issue that for most has never been and would never be an issue. They have selfishly misappropriated or, more generously, misconstrued 'violence' to include spanking in the everyday meaning of the word for most of the world's parents.

But spanking is certainly not violence. It is almost always done with good intention: parents are not intending to hurt their own children, merely to protect them. There is a marvellous Yiddish word that captures beautifully the essence of how the vast majority of the world's parents really interpret so-called legalised violence towards our own children every day: a 'potch', which falls somewhere between a hard tap and a mild smack on the backside, hand-delivered out of love and concern (and perhaps Jewish anxiety) over a child's wellbeing. It's an extension of the Jewish mother wringing her hands with concern over her child.

Those who are genuinely violent towards their children should obviously be dealt with. However, a potch is *not* violence, and is far from the 'cruel or degrading forms of legalised violence against children' that the UN and others with a warped view of normal parental spanking declare it to be. It is hardly worth dignifying such an unnecessary debate.

If legislators and social engineers are truly concerned with protecting children from the most damaging aspects of parenting, why, for example, is there no move to outlaw cold, unaffectionate, uninvolved parenting? Why is there no attempt to criminalise the divorced mother who prevents her child from seeing his father? Both of these are far more harmful to a child's development than a slap on the wrist could ever be.

William James, one of the world's original psychologists, long ago suspected that sticks and stones may break your bones but words – or at least a lack of them – will *always* hurt you: 'If no one turned round when we entered, answered when we spoke, or minded what we did, but if every person we met "cut us dead", and acted as if we were non-existing things, a kind of rage and impotent despair would ere long well up in us, from which the cruellest bodily tortures would be a relief.'[2]

James was correct, and, in fact, a lack of words can hurt a child more than corporal punishment. New research is finding that our hurt feelings far outlast memories of physical pain. Those overly concerned about the effects of giving our child a smack or slap on the wrist may be interested in the study 'When Hurt Will Not Heal', published in *Psychological Science*, which examined how the emotional consequences of being criticised, cold-shouldered or neglected (social pain) compare with being hurt physically, and concluded: 'Individuals can re-live and re-experience social pain more easily and more intensely than physical pain ... Specifically, whereas both types of pain are agonisingly intense, physical pain is typically short-lived, whereas social pain may last for ever.' Interestingly, the emotional pain of being ostracised or excluded from a social situation activates the same section of the brain – the dorsal anterior cingulate cortex – that detects and experiences physical pain from being slapped on the wrist.

While physical pain teaches a child not to repeat actions that damage their bodies, social pain may be useful to ensure that they follow certain rules of interaction. But the fact that this pain is so enduring and can potentially lead to emotional problems or depression may be an unintended side-effect. 'The evolution of the cerebral cortex certainly improved the ability of human beings to create and adapt; to function in and with groups, communities, and culture; and to respond to pain associated with social interactions,' the authors of the study wrote. 'However, the cerebral cortex may also have had an unintended effect of allowing humans to re-live, re-experience, and suffer from social pain.'[3] Although the American Association of Psychoanalysts in Private Practice and Doing Very Nicely may appreciate the re-living of social pain, the main bodies concerned with our children's wellbeing seem more worried about the deep-seated damage caused by a slap on the wrist.

Back in the real world, the majority of the world's parents don't have to think about this and merely want to reserve the right to spank only if their children misbehave in a most serious and perilous situation. Most of us realise that it's usually not possible to stop and have a deep and meaningful discussion about thermodynamics and its relationship to epithelial destruction as our child's hand is about to touch a red-hot cooker burner. A slap on the hand may cause him to hesitate next time before going to the stove, but is unlikely to destroy him emotionally or prevent him from becoming a chef when he grows up.

Yet some continue to disagree ardently. Britain's Global Initiative to End All Corporal Punishment of Children sees a slap on the wrist as 'violence to children' to be considered and eradicated like 'domestic violence to women'. The Council of Europe, a forty-seven-country body that is supposed to promote civil liberties, launched the 'Raise your hand against smacking' initiative in 2008. In the United States, on the Pacific coast, there's the San Francisco Bay Area Center for Nonviolent Communication, and on the East coast, there's EPOCH (End Physical Punishment of Children), which sponsors a national 'SpankOut Day' every year on 30 April. There is even an international spanking ranking, replete with bottom hit counts: 74 per cent of students surveyed in Tanzania said they were spanked, the highest rate among thirty-two nations studied.

This is hardly meant to trivialise genuine violence against children or to allow the spanking of babies. Nor does it recommend reactionary punishment in favour of communicating with and teaching our children, and rewarding their good behaviour.

Pushover parents

Nowadays, it's popular and almost mandatory to stress fair-sounding concepts such as choice, autonomy, 'freedom to want', 'freedom to choose', 'self-expression'. Conformity to boundaries for our children and the required discipline to achieve this has been undermined in other oblique ways. For example, viewing spelling and grammar as the overly restrictive table manners of the written word, John Wells, Emeritus Professor of Phonetics at University College London and president of the Spelling Society, has blamed our growing literacy problems on the 'burden' the English spelling system places on children. Bringing the mountain to Mohammed, he suggests, 'Let's allow people greater freedom to spell logically . . . Text messaging, email and Internet chat rooms are showing us the way forward for English.' This is surely the institutional academic equivalent of wanting to be best friends with our children, as opposed to being their superior who knows better and is in a position to correct them. Presumably, this is why he is called Professor and our children are called pupils, and why he can mark our children's papers but they cannot mark his.

I often walk my own and other people's children to school. As an honorary school-gate mother, I've had a great deal of time to observe modern parents who, when they say 'No' to their child, say it almost with a sense of apology in their voice and a lack of conviction in their demeanour, which often reeks of acquiescence. I also hear a measured, cautious tone of voice in bystanders, police and teachers when they have to confront badly behaved children and teenagers. Unlike parents, they have been forced to stand aside by fashionable laws that prevent them from exerting their authority.

I've also come across many examples of the tail wagging the dog on the issue of controlling how much television young children watch. I recently published a book and a biology paper on the physiological effects of screen viewing on children and was contacted in this connection by various writers on children and parenting issues. I was asked how parents can control the amount of television their children watch – a question to which the answer seemed fairly straightforward, to me at least: 'The most important thing is not to put a television in a young child's bedroom. Keep it in the sitting room, and make it clear that *you* control when and how much they watch. If they're under the age of three, the medical evidence suggests you should keep them away from television until we know more about why certain symptoms are linked to early television viewing,' and so on. However, my response was met with some consternation, and I was asked whether it was really as simple as telling a child they can't have a television in their room or they can't watch it; there were other issues to consider, I was told, and sometimes you have to negotiate.

The general impression I was left with by the many journalists and experts I spoke to – who were also parents – was that they appeared to be scared of their own young children's reaction to being told, 'No.' And whether liberal, left or conservative, they came across as people who wanted to ensure that they could get on with whatever they needed to do at home, while their children were occupied in front of a television screen.

This is all a part of a selfish belief that we should negotiate with our children because it seems more democratic and egalitarian – and it's also just plain nicer to endear ourselves to them, as opposed to challenging and upsetting them. This also reflects a misplaced concern that to demand our children's compliance, through compulsion if necessary, will in some way be counterproductive and even harmful, quashing their character and preventing them from expressing themselves.

This tolerant approach was sometimes thought of as a 'child-centred' approach. However, we now have to ask: did this notion really place the child as the centrepiece of his parents' concerns in the way intended, or did it put the child in the driving seat, sending their development in the wrong direction because it seemed an easier ride in the short term?

We'd all prefer to enlist our child's co-operation and even

endear ourselves to them in the process – but parenting also involves the not-so-feelgood aspects. At a time when parents are older and more overworked than ever before, confrontation and punishment are not the first things that spring to mind when your child defies you. Time poverty, divorce and separation have drawn many of us parents unknowingly into a compensation culture. Our parental guilt continues to be assuaged by allowing extra tolerance towards our children's unacceptable behaviour, coupled with greater indulgence. And it's being noticed everywhere.

From top-drawer elite private schools to the gold-chains-no-brains culture of holding pens masquerading as schools, those at the coalface are beginning to speak out about parenting and boundaries. The principal of Cheltenham Ladies' College and president of the Girls' Schools Association laments, 'the forgotten craft of parenting ... They are lacking confidence in themselves as parents – when did we forget the craft of parenting, forget that your daughter is not there to be your best friend?' These perceptions and sentiments are classless. The General Secretary of the teachers' union Voice uses his to warn: 'Somehow, we have got to break this downward spiral of parenting skills. Teachers are increasingly forced to discipline bad behaviour and take on the role of bringing up children because parents too often pander to their demands.' At the behest of the West Midlands Police, in nine primary schools in Birmingham, children as young as eight are being taught 'anger management' through 'conflict and resolution training' as compensation for a lack of parental boundaries at home.

Children at both ends of the socioeconomic spectrum are suffering from a lack of moral and behavioural boundaries. At the low end, children are joining gangs who *do* provide the strong role-modelling structures and boundaries that have disappeared from family and civic life. The more privileged, on the other hand, binge drink, self-harm, pop pills (including anti-depressants) as never before, while managing, at the same time, to be disrespectful.

A lack of boundaries is also showing up in other unexpected places. A growing number of researchers believe that many children who are categorised at school as having attention deficit hyperactivity disorder (ADHD) are, in fact, just badly behaved. They suggest that such children are disruptive in lessons or refuse to co-operate with teachers because they've simply been raised with a lack of boundaries.

With boundaries in mind, I am interested in an analysis of empirical evidence for what the researchers call 'religious pro-sociality' – showing how being religious may make us nicer, better behaved and more altruistic, rather than selfish. The authors believe: 'One reason we now have large co-operative societies may be that some aspects of religion – such as out-sourcing costly social policing duties to all-powerful Gods – made societies work more co-operatively in the past.'[4]

Psychiatric studies on the effects of religion have found that children with stronger religious faith may benefit from a protective effect against depression, while stronger religious faith among us adults is linked with a lower prevalence of depression and greater optimism.

As an agnostic who has never taken tea with a vicar – or a mullah for that matter – I must admit to feeling rather down in the dumps about these findings. None the less, what is interesting for me are some of the beneficial effects of existing within moral and behavioural limits patrolled by the divine enforcer; they serve as an example of how living within boundaries, knowing that there is a figure of authority to oversee us, is generally good for us.

'Natural justice'

It certainly isn't children who have an aversion to punishment with a capital P. They seem to possess a sense of what we could loosely call natural justice and I'm quite happy to exploit this disposition whenever naughtiness – sorry, I mean 'inappropriate behaviour' – takes place in our house. I have noticed that when one of my young children hurts the other and the victim can't get even and cries, I can bring an almost instant peace to the house by asking the injured party and any corroborative witnesses, 'What happened?' Once it's clear that the offending sibling is guilty, I ask the aggrieved, 'How many pokes should I give him – three, five or eight?' They have to stop crying in order to calculate, and invariably they say, 'Twenty-seven!' I then offer further options to my bespoke retribution service, asking, 'Where should he get the pokes: back, belly or foot?' The victim then has to concentrate further to assess which area will be most effective before deciding. The guilty party meanwhile, listening to all of this and knowing what is coming their way, tries to curl up and minimise their target area, but I deliver the pokes anyway, counting deliberately out loud, so the victim can hear justice being done. There have been cases where one of my children has perverted the course of natural justice or framed the other, but as it's not capital punishment, the miscarriage of natural justice is something we can all live with.

The UN will be saddened to learn that my children suffer other 'cruel or degrading forms of punishment' that the UN Convention on the Rights of the Child may have overlooked: the use of cryogenic corporal punishment. This new disturbing approach to childcare came to me one evening in the kitchen while I was trying to make dinner. As I held a frozen salmon, my two young boys were misbehaving and trying it on with me. So I announced, 'The next person to throw that ball in the kitchen is going to get a frozen fish down their trousers!' It only took two minutes for the youngest to test the boundaries before I caught him, kept my promise and slotted the frozen creature straight down the back of his trousers. He ran around half-yelping and half-giggling and, although this is obviously not what Captain Birdseye may have intended, frozen fish have

become an integral part of my 'behavioural modification' reper-
toire. My wife reminds me that this is not what she meant when
she said we need to make sure the children get enough omega 3s,
and demands my assurance that after justice has been served, the
fish is thoroughly cooked. (There are variations on the theme
involving frozen peas.)

Some cynics might argue that twenty-five years from now my
children will develop a frozen fish fetish, ending up either on a
psychotherapist's couch, or on his knees in the confines of a
bordello, begging, 'Please ... slap me again with that frozen
fish and tell me I'm a naughty boy!' But I'm willing to take the
risk. (And I suspect my literary agent sees the potential for a
whole new genre of cookery-book-meets-misery-memoir emerging from my son's trauma.)

The idea of a predictable fair system governed with authority,
reinforcing the boundaries and constructs in our child's life, provides them with a sense of coherence. Indeed, restrictions and
consequences, far from diminishing a child's world, are liberating. But parents, and society as a whole, feel ambivalent about
embracing the idea of punishment too enthusiastically. We have
been endlessly encouraged to negotiate and certainly to avoid
being punitive in our responses to crossed boundaries and
broken rules.

Many people see punishment as primitive and atavistic, and
therefore damaging to our children, perhaps breaking their
spirit. Some 'experts' emphasise the philosophical differences
between punishment and discipline, seeing them as entirely different concepts. Punishment is considered nothing more than
taking action against your child as a payback for their behaviour, while discipline is about guiding your child and teaching
them to understand limits at home or in other settings. Yet in
reality, one does not preclude the other; judicious punishment is
often a necessary part of discipline and can take many different
forms. Real-time punishment, such as shouting at our child at

exactly the point at which they are doing something bad – sorry, again, I mean 'inappropriate' – may instil discipline, guiding them and teaching them to understand limits at home or in other settings.

Like smacking, punishment has to some extent been fetishised and tainted with a feeling that it is the first cousin of sadism. To punish, especially if it involves 'legalised violence' (a potch) or a menacing shout and shake, is, it is thought, to revert to a more primitive way of thinking and feeling that's best confined to the pages of *Lord of the Flies*. Whether it involves dealing with criminals or our own children, punishment that expresses our own anger is not considered acceptable. It used to be called expressive justice, and for centuries it was a central tenet to civic life and government in Europe and the American colonies, until we evolved beyond such basic instincts to become as civilised . . . as we are today. Punishment served to vent the community's outrage and exact revenge in public through defined rituals of retribution in which the whole community participated. Expressive justice satisfied a desire for symbolic reassertions of authority and accountability.

More recently, however, we have focused far more on techniques that will alter someone's future behaviour, without stepping back to see that while a symbolic reassertion of authority and accountability does indeed have great therapeutic value for the victim of the wrongdoing (and perhaps the person doling out the punishment), the wrongdoer also learns and is reassured by this clear system of justice. And others learn by observing this process. There is certainly nothing wrong with our children knowing – *feeling* – our anger being vented through their punishment, provided they know – *feel* – that we love them. A key part of their social and emotional development is to learn that their behaviour has direct effects on the emotions and behavioural reactions of others. As parents, we are introducing them to this concept in a controlled and loving way.

A recurring theme in the criminal justice system is that victims are left unable to express real anger and are made to feel that venting their outrage and wanting retribution and to reassert their authority – to *feel* the formerly all-powerful criminal physically and emotionally disempowered – is infantile, right-wing and politically incorrect. The notion that there is a therapeutic benefit to this process for the victim and a social medicine for society is too uncomfortable to be discussed seriously.

Both disciplining our children and criminal justice have become disconnected, sanitised affairs in which we're told that it's more advanced, sophisticated and effective to objectify our child or our attacker in order to best achieve 'behavioural change' or 'rehabilitation'. We've moved on from punishment. Yet the refrain 'there's no justice' that we so often hear from victims or their families, is a cry for these 'unacceptable' psychological elements to be included in the criminal justice system.

Parenting my own children has informed my understanding of punishment immeasurably. So has the Islamic Republic of Iran. Irrespective of my own feelings about capital punishment, what I saw in the heart of the ancient Persian city of Isfahan forced me to reconsider my Western sensibilities and arrogance at the presumption that I live in a more highly evolved and civilised culture.

As I strolled down Nazar Street, I noticed people casually pointing at and discussing a crane in the distance that struck me as rather unremarkable. I thought that perhaps Iranians simply had a love of cranes – one of those cultural things that went unmentioned in the Lonely Planet guidebook. When I asked a young man why the crane was of such interest, he said, 'Look, a child murderer is there', at which point I realised that a body was dangling at the end of a long rope tied to the top of the crane. The man also told me that victims' families can watch public lashings of the attacker. As Hossein Zabhi, Iran's Deputy

State Public Prosecutor, explains: 'We can't deny a victim's family the legal right to ask for Islamic Qasas, or eye-for-eye retribution.'[5]

My friends and colleagues understandably dismiss this as barbaric, but the relevant point is that at least the Iranians have incorporated an *emotional* element to boundaries and punishment that we have rejected to our cost – namely, the inclusion of anger, along with a symbolic reassertion of authority and accountability in dealing with wrongdoing. Not that I'd recommend keeping a gallows and bullwhip in the back garden as an alternative to negotiating with your child.

Terms and conditions apply

There isn't a one-size-fits-all approach to boundaries and discipline because children, their parents and their circumstances all differ. While sex differences will be discussed in more detail in Chapter Four, boys are, to start with, generally more physically aggressive, difficult and challenging. They're also less verbal and more impulsive. One simple reason for this may be that boys may not listen as well as girls because their hearing in the frequency range critical to speech discrimination isn't as good from birth. Girls are designed to be people-oriented, while boys are more action-oriented. Boys also push boundaries and are greater risk-takers. However, the complexity of girls catches up with parents during adolescence. They have an infuriating way of using nuance, smiles and acts of kindness to insult and challenge.

And then there are behavioural genetics. A recent study published by the National Academy of Sciences on the 'heritability of cooperative behavior' concluded: 'We urge social scientists to take seriously the idea that differences in peer and parental socialisation are not the only forces that influence variation in cooperative behaviour.'[6] And a new study in the *Journal of Abnormal Child Psychology*, which tracked 1863 children from birth to the age of thirteen, found that more challenging infants develop into more challenging and difficult children with conduct problems from the ages of four to thirteen. Genetic differences in infant temperament are evident right from the start, and they found that infant 'fussiness was a stronger predictor of conduct problems in boys, whereas fearfulness was a stronger predictor in girls'. However, parenting style in the first year of the infant's life also has an important influence. Infants whose mothers gave them a lot of stimulation by talking and reading to them and taking them out of the house during the first year of life were less likely to have conduct problems later.[7] So, while it's not our fault that a child may have inherited a more contrary nature, we're left with the responsibility to work with the temperament Mother Nature has dealt them.

But as parents, we too come with conditions: our own temperaments influence our parenting style and interact with our children's. And biological factors, such as our gender and age, affect how short our fuse is and how much energy we have for confrontation when our children cross boundaries.

Family structure brings further issues. Are we single, or separated or divorced. And, if the latter, was it an acrimonious or non-acrimonious split? A single mother trying to enforce boundaries with a boy, or a single father trying to make sense of the subtleties of his daughter's insurrection, is likely to have a very different experience from a single parent whose child is the same sex as them. And then size matters too: two parents with one child have more latitude than two parents with four children or one parent with three. It's fine to expect parents in each of these families to adhere to a standard, but the reality is that when the ratio of children to parent is high, efficiency becomes an issue: controlling a mob of four young boys is quite a different affair from dealing with one girl who, by the age of six, has reached the age of reason.

The number of children, the number of parents around to

parent them, the ages of the children and *their* sexes . . . the modulating factors go on. But still the general principle of boundaries and consequences remains constant.

Furthermore, as you can see, the earlier we start the better. Our children arrive fully loaded with genetic baggage that, as their handlers, we have to handle. While the terrible twos may be trying now, the way this stage is handled can make life a lot easier or more difficult several years down the line. We may empathise with a child's desire to assert his or her own will, but we are still the parent, and should always act like it. The terrible twos actually represent a child's first attempt at becoming independent, but this doesn't mean that temper tantrums are acceptable. Bad behaviour should not be accepted or encouraged.

We can offer our children choices, but we cannot allow their preferences to run our lives. As parents, we must still provide structure and support for our children, even if it doesn't taste good. Though it may take years, our children will appreciate it later, especially when they have children of their own. As is the case with authority, limits make children feel safe and secure. And while they may not act or look happy when we impose a consequence, setting limits and enforcing them shows children that they actually matter to us – that they are loved enough to motivate a tired, overworked parent to deal with them, as opposed to taking the easier option and conceding. The relevance of this spreads far and wide: clear and consistently enforced limits and boundaries teach our children the protocol of life, so they can grow up, fit in and cope.

Praising our children by describing to them precisely what it is we think they've done well is, of course, the staple diet of cultivating good behaviour and steering them away from unacceptable behaviour. Yet that is only one side – the jolly side – of parenting. Children expect an overriding environment of natural justice, and you are responsible and entitled to administer this . . . without feeling guilty about it. Failure to do so is a successful way to produce a spoilt child who will become even more challenging and difficult, therefore requiring still more energy to deal with. The choice is yours.

While 'experts' and other concerned bodies are preoccupied with techniques and the specifics of discipline, what isn't being fully recognised is that whether we call it discipline or punishment, it is our relationship with our children that makes all the difference. If our children feel secure, considered, cared for and that they have connections with us, then the UN and others needn't worry about the supposedly soul-destroying effects of discipline and punishment.

In the meantime, I look forward to a reversal of the current laws and associated social stigma surrounding boundaries and discipline. Parents who do not discipline and, if absolutely necessary, smack their children, should be considered shoddier parents who are failing their children and society. It's a terrible shame we can't tar and feather them.

Four

PC Parenting

Mothers are not fathers; fathers are not mothers

It seems hard to believe that until the eighteenth century, child-rearing manuals in America were in most cases addressed to fathers, not mothers. But as industrialisation began to take men away from home in order to work, fathers could not be in both places at the same time. Family life in the nineteenth century saw what historians describe as the feminisation of the domestic sphere and the marginalisation of the father as a parent. By the 1830s, child-rearing manuals were increasingly directed at mothers, deploring the father's absence from the home. In 1900 one writer in *Harper's Bazaar* observed, 'The suburban husband and father is almost entirely a Sunday institution', while other popular magazine articles sported titles such as, 'It's Time Father Got Back in the Family'. In *The Father's Book* (1834), Theodore Dwight urged men to resume their responsibilities at home, lamenting that the father, 'eager in the pursuit of business, toils early and late, and finds no time to fulfil . . . duties to his children'.[1]

Today, the quaint little cry, 'Wait till your father gets home!'

is heard less frequently and carries less influence than in years gone by. This is not merely because fewer fathers are now coming home at all, but because when they do walk through the front door, they are expected to think and behave differently from their predecessors. As part of the move towards increasingly 'progressive parenting' we've been encouraged to consider parenting a more genderless affair. Many of us have come to parenting in what is a time of emotional correctness; the fashion to play down our sex differences in many areas includes the way in which we relate to our own children. There has been a misplaced emphasis on sexual equality as opposed to *equivalence* and this has come at a cost both to our children and to us.

One of the more colourful examples of this seems like something straight out of a 1970s student feminist newspaper, the Starsky and Hutch episode of sexual equality. This new study entitled, 'New Fathers and Mothers as Gender Troublemakers? Exploring Discursive Constructions of Heterosexual Parenthood and their Subversive Potential', would have Germaine Greer taking a fire extinguisher to her burning bra. Yet studies like this do confer an ambient degree of credibility and legitimacy to the convenient notion that as mothers and fathers we are reasonably interchangeable, but we just don't fully realise it yet:

> Current constructions of heterosexual parenthood in Western societies seem to be trapped in a change-retention dilemma. Many elements have changed, but many others have stayed the same . . . Parenthood is still constructed along the heterosexual gender binary that equates women with mothers and men with fathers.[2]

Children, however, are having none of it. In fact, our children *need* us as mothers and fathers to behave differently, and, if we don't, it will be to their detriment.

In an out-of-the-mouths-of-babes demonstration of truth and reality, scientists have documented the obvious. However, nowadays, it is ever-more necessary to state the obvious to prevent the abnormal from becoming the norm for our children just because it may be convenient for someone. In 2009, the study 'Boys Will Be Boys; Cows Will Be Cows: Children's Essentialist Reasoning About Gender Categories and Animal Species', found that our children are born with an inherent presumption that we as males and females, mothers and fathers, are inherently different and that our differences come from the inside, not from society – we are born with them. Five- and six-year-olds saw men and women as being the equivalent of two completely different species of animal.[3] I'll let you guess who's the cow and who's the pig.

Complementarity

Research consistently shows that mothers and fathers parent differently and in ways that matter enormously. Ignoring these profound differences may be convenient and beneficial to some modern parents and the politically correct, but their views are insignificant when compared to their children's wellbeing.

For example, children may benefit when mothers and fathers react differently to their negative emotions, such as distress, anxiety or anger; when both parents are supportive, they may actually prevent their child from handling these negative emotions. The researchers in one study suggest that if, for instance, a child becomes anxious or upset about losing a favourite toy, he ends up involved in fewer conflicts with his friends and with a better understanding of his negative emotions when one parent provides little support and the other provides more. For example, the mother may intervene by hugging their child and helping to look for the toy, while the father hangs back and is available if needed.

The findings highlight the importance of understanding how mothers and fathers together may influence their children's ability to understand and manage emotions. By moving beyond a 'mother-only' model and examining the joint contributions that mothers and fathers make to their children's wellbeing, researchers, clinicians and early childhood educators will be better positioned to design and implement interventions aimed at fostering healthy social and emotional development.[4]

I don't mention this research in order to encourage mothers and fathers to make a concerted effort to react differently to their children's dilemmas or experiences. It's intended, simply, to allow parenting differences, particularly male/female ones, to express themselves without reservation, especially the behaviour of fathers.

And by reacting differently, parents should not worry about undermining one another, sending their child mixed messages or creating an opportunity to play one parent off against the other. Parents should be comfortable about parenting more instinctively.

Yet in many families, something valuable has been eroded in the revolution in parenting – some uniquely male contribution that is vital for raising our children and which dictates that fathers should be more than assistant mothers.

In all of the most remote and unrelated parts of the world I've travelled to, the people from different cultures, tribes, religions and histories all have one thing in common: they assume men and women/mothers and fathers are fundamentally different – end of story. But there's one experience in particular that neatly encapsulates the enormous gulf between men and women. I came home one afternoon to find our electrician, Jack, standing on a ladder in our kitchen, repairing the ceiling light. At the foot of the ladder stood my five-year-old daughter who, pointing up at Jack, told me rather nonchalantly, 'Daddy, Jack isn't a boy any more, he's a lady now.' And she was right. Jack – now Jacquie – had indeed acquired make-up and big hair and lost one or two things in the process. Or, as he explained to my wife, 'I've had all me bits removed.'

In New York, London, Paris, Tokyo, Sydney and beyond, transsexuals are willing to pay a fortune to undergo surgery and endure punishing hormone regimes in order to change from one side to the other. Presumably, they too suspect that men and women are profoundly different.

And yet there is an ongoing industry continuing to investigate this open question, along with a manufactured 'debate' suggesting that men and women are essentially very similar. This stems from the legacy of the 1960s which was concerned that revealing differences between one group and another (blacks/whites, Jews/Gentiles, chauvinists/wimmin) inevitably leads to one group being seen as superior and the other inferior. Biological predispositions are seen as constricting hindrances to the feelgood view that you can be anything you wanna be and do anything you wanna do.

I often marvel at how we manage to coo about 'celebrating diversity', while in the next breath we gush that 'we're all the same'. Bureaucrats are too busy embracing diversity to bother looking it up in a dictionary, or even to stop and think for that matter. Diverse means 'different' and different does not exactly mean 'the same'. We can't have it both ways; if we really are to 'celebrate diversity', we'd better acknowledge what our differences actually are before we start celebrating them.

A new generation of female neuroscientists does not seem to find the idea of profound biological differences between male and female in the slightest bit threatening. In fact, they are desperate to understand as much as possible about these differences in order 'to guide the development of sex-specific treatments for these devastating brain disorders'. Researchers at Yale University

School of Medicine with the most unmanly names of Kelly, Carolyn and Julie, have published a major twenty-six-year review of 'Sex Differences in Brain Structure, Function, and Chemistry'. They concluded, very matter-of-factly, that in all of these areas, 'there are important differences that distinguish the male from the female brain'.[5]

In a piquant twist of irony, while these three female researchers were busy at Yale delineating all of the vast differences between male and female brains, up the road at Harvard the twenty-seventh President of Harvard University, Larry Summers, was forced to resign for merely *asking* whether there may be any intrinsic differences between men and women: 'You have to be careful in attributing things to socialisation . . . That's what we would prefer to believe, but these are things that need to be studied.' Unfortunately, an ardent feminist academic sitting just ten feet away from Summers became enraged, closed her computer, put on her coat and walked out. She explained that she had to leave the lecture because if she hadn't, she would have 'either blacked out or thrown up'. She also said: 'When [Mr Summers] started talking about innate differences in aptitude between men and women, I just couldn't breathe because this kind of bias makes me physically ill.'[6]

It was pointed out by some observers that things have come full circle. At one time, women used to claim that indecent language would cause them to grow ill or faint. Now feminists are using the same ploy to silence ideologically unacceptable ideas and to intimidate the intellectually inquisitive.

I was surprised to read an article by the neuroscientist and highly acclaimed author Professor Steven Pinker, now the Family Professor of Psychology at Harvard, in which he admitted that for about fifteen years he intentionally avoided researching or teaching anything like this that might have a political dimension: '. . . a student recently asked me if there was evidence for biologically based differences between men's and women's minds. I flushed and sweated, fearing a riot would break out if I answered truthfully ... I explained that these topics were incendiary.'[7] To think that a man of Professor Pinker's stature should literally sweat and fear when answering an academic question truthfully raises extremely important questions. How is it that the wrath of the politically correct few can be allowed to prevail unchecked? Why did Professor Pinker spend fifteen years evading what in most cultures are rather unremarkable questions about the human mind? Moreover, how many other less well-known academics have behaved or continue to behave similarly?

The academic industry supplying us with the latest news of our differences-but-with-sameness has done well to reassure those unrestrained by common sense that whether we as men and women really are fundamentally different remains an unanswered question. A typical interview in *Psychology Tomorrow* follows a comfortable recognised form:

Psychology Tomorrow's Editor-at-Slim Lisa Rumpelstiltskin-Hack recently caught up with Professor Martha Toadstool-Fink at Bottom's Up Open-Minded University's Department of Gender Realignment, who explained the latest developments in her research: 'We're terribly excited about the latest intriguing differences we've discovered between males and females – and the many, many papers I've managed to publish as a result of our findings. [This declaratory revelation is invariably followed by what has become an off-the-shelf caveat:] Of course men and women are far more similar than they are different, so we can't generalise or assume that men and women are different. More research is needed to investigate the intriguing differences between males and females that aren't really that different after all. Research funds can be donated to me at ...'

Of course, Professor Toadstool-Fink is right to the extent that as two sexes, we each have two eyes, ears, arms and legs. But perhaps I shouldn't generalise.

Those of you who thought this type of juvenile American debate was from a bygone era should consider that the implications of this rarefied argument are wide-ranging and have a trickle-down effect into areas such as parenting, divorce, child custody/residence and contact. Women and men are created differently, and we must assume this to be the case until it is shown to be otherwise. It's time that the burden of proof was placed firmly on the social engineers. If men and women are different, it stands to reason that they will do many things in different ways. Parenting just happens to be one item in a very long list, and the most important one.

Kyle Pruett, Clinical Professor of Child Psychiatry and Director of Medical Studies at the Yale University Child Study Center, Yale University School of Medicine, has a consuming interest in the complementary, necessary differences between mothers and fathers. To Pruett, fathers matter simply because 'fathers do not mother'.[8] There is great concern that genderless parenting is more than merely a stylistic personal choice for the social fashionista – fathers should now be actively expected to be more than pale imitations of mothers. Professor Jerrold Lee Shapiro of the Graduate Department of Counseling Psychology, Santa Clara University, has spent much of his career trying to celebrate the mother/father difference. 'If you become Mr Mom, the family has a mother and an assistant mother. That isn't what good fathers are doing today.'[9]

In a position statement on behalf of Texas A&M University entitled 'What Fathers Contribute to Child Development', Linda D. Ladd, now Professor of Family Studies at Texas Women's University, states: 'Having the experience of two involved parents adds variety and dimension to the child's experience of the world.'[10] For our children to develop fully, we should, ideally, ensure sure that they have daily access to the different and complementary ways in which mothers and fathers parent. Generally, mothers and fathers parent differently, play differently, communicate differently, prepare children for life differently. Fathers push limits; mothers encourage security. Fathers provide a look at the world of men; mothers, the world of women. Fathers and mothers teach respect for the opposite sex.

And mothers and fathers discipline differently, in a combination which yields what is sometimes described as justice tempered by mercy. Fathers help children see that particular attitudes and behaviours have certain consequences. Professor Carol Gilligan, the American feminist, ethicist, psychologist and visiting professor with the University of Cambridge (Centre for Gender Studies), finds that mothers tend to emphasise sympathy, care and help, and focus on relationships as they discipline. In contrast, fathers put emphasis on justice, fairness and duty, with a focus on rules. It now seems that it is in combination that these complementary styles of discipline are most effective. Fathers tend to observe and enforce rules systematically and sternly, which teaches children the objectivity and consequences of right and wrong. Mothers tend more towards grace and sympathy in the midst of disobedience, which provides a sense of hopefulness. Either of these approaches by themselves is not ideal, but in tandem, they create a synergistic, healthy balance.

The developmental psychologist Erik Erikson described father love and mother love as being qualitatively different too. Fathers 'love more dangerously' because their love is more 'expectant, more instrumental' than a mother's. The expression 'only their mother could love them' implies that a mother's love is unconditional compared to a father's, which could be considered more qualified, more tied to performance; mothers are worried about the infant's survival, fathers about future success. Many people remember the 'Iron Lady', Prime Minister

Margaret Thatcher, crying in public when she learnt that her flamboyant, errant son Mark was reported lost in the Sahara Desert. (Those unfamiliar with the Thatchers can be reassured to know that Mark returned and continued to embarrass his mother for years to come.)

Children usually learn from their mother more of an awareness of their emotional side, while from their father they learn how to live in society, to become socially viable. With respect to spoiling our children, a mother's ability to help her child cultivate empathy can enable them to connect their behaviours emotionally to their effects on others, while a father can help encourage their ability to connect their behaviours with consequences. But there is some overlap. Linda Ladd points out that: 'Fathers who actively play with their children appear to reinforce the notion of emotional self-control in their children and help their children learn to recognise the emotional cues of others.'[10]

There are obviously exceptions to all of the above, but mothers and fathers generally fall into relatively well-defined roles that children can relate to, roles that complement rather than militate against each other. In a properly functioning family, the outcome is more likely to be a well-adjusted, better behaved young adult. The unique and vital contributions of men and women as parents should be cherished not denied.

Aural authority

One of the main dimensions of a father's influence over his child is the pitch of his voice. Many mothers, including my own wife, lament, 'Why is it that when *you* shout at them they listen and do what they're supposed to, but when I do it they ignore me?!' (In our case, this also applies to the way our dog responds to my voice as opposed to my wife's.)

Whether an oink or a grunt, like a father's physical size, his voice carries more weight and menace, more authority. This is the sonic landscape of parenting and one of the elephant-in-the-corner explanations of why fathers affect children differently and significantly.

I just read an interesting study on which type of emergency fire alarm sounds and voices are most effective in waking sleeping children, that reported: 'The male voice alarm was the most successful of all signals . . .'[11]

At a primitive level, children respond more to the authority of their father's voice because male voices are inextricably linked with the sex that is naturally more aggressive, dominating and violent. Journals such as *Biological Psychology* take this point seriously, carrying studies such as, 'Relationships between vocal characteristics and body size and shape in human males: an evolutionary explanation for a deep male voice.' There is a strong relationship between a man's 'fundamental frequency' (depth of speaking voice) and his body shape and weight: the lower the voice the bigger the boy. And the same is true of his 'formant dispersion' (harmonic shape of his voice). This is referred to as '. . . the size exaggeration theory of laryngeal descent',[12] and the researchers suggest that 'male voices may have deepened over the course of evolution in order to signal dominance'. The 'wait-till-your-father-gets-home' threat is now being put under the microscope to discover what fuels its power and authority. The relationship between testosterone and vocal frequencies in human males finds a 'relationship between circulating levels of testosterone and fundamental frequency, with higher testosterone indicating lower fundamental frequency'.[13]

It isn't surprising that professional or ambitious women appear to have lowered the pitch of their speaking voice over the past fifty years. A comparison of women's voices between 1945 and 1993 reveals that they deepened significantly in the second half of the century. But the trend for women to imitate the deep voices of actresses and television presenters was first observed in the 1970s. One study found that women were tending to pitch their voices approximately two-thirds of an octave higher than men's, rather than the more usual one octave. And audio archivists have noted the deepening trend as high-powered female politicians and television broadcasters are being encouraged to lower their pitch.[14]

In order to gain authority, and control her cabinet of little boys, Lady Thatcher was famously advised by spin doctors to exchange her shrill tones for a deeper delivery. The British Voice Association refers to: 'The descent of the Thatcher voice from young political debutante to unwilling dowager duchess . . .'[15]

From infancy, children recognise and classify voices into male and female categories.[16] And new studies even find sexual inequality in their grey matter: 'The perception of male and female voices activates distinct brain regions.'[17]

Encouraging men to tone down their voices and become meeker is staring a parental gift horse in the mouth. A father's voice is probably the most under-recognised resource in shaping our children's behaviour, keeping order and preventing our children from becoming spoilt. Dad shouldn't keep mum.

Vive la différence

The aim of the information and examples provided above is to rid parenting of the stifling sexual politics that have crept in unnoticed, freeing parents to fulfil their roles in a more uncontrived, less politically defined way.

Hopefully, mothers and fathers may be more understanding when they see their partner dealing with their child in a different way from the one they would choose. Conversely, just because most heterosexual and many gay couples display general variations in parenting style doesn't mean anyone should engineer differences in the way they and their partner parent so that they conform to the norm.

We need to reclaim some of the natural differences between mothers and fathers from the domain of too much discussion, thought and sexual politics, and allow our intuitive side – honed over millions of years – to take over.

Five

Delegated Parenting

How institutional daycare contributes to spoilt children

By the twenty-sixth century, in Aldous Huxley's *Brave New World*, having your child the good old-fashioned way through sex and giving birth has been completely done away with. Marriage is considered an anti-social filthy joke and any mention of natural birth or pregnancy is most repulsive and vulgar. Instead, in what could be described as the ultimate in progressive parenting, children are decanted and raised in 'hatcheries' and 'conditioning centres'. The idea of a 'family' is revolting and the hypnopaedic proverb 'everyone belongs to everyone else' is repeated often. Or as the World Controller of Western Europe describes us historical whores: 'Human beings used to be . . . Well, they used to be viviparous . . . (For you must remember that in those days of gross viviparous reproduction, children were always brought up by their parents and not in State Conditioning Centres.)'

And if the thought of reproductive sex produces a palpable nausea at just its mention, the parent–child relationship is the unmentionable, while the greatest depravity is reserved for the most ghastly of bygone phenomena, the mother–child bond:

> Just try to realize it . . . Try to realize what it was like to have a viviparous mother . . . Try to imagine what 'living with one's family' meant . . . And do you know what a 'home' was? . . .
>
> . . . as squalid psychically as physically . . . reeking with emotion. What suffocating intimacies . . . Maniacally, the mother brooded over her children (*her* children) . . . brooded over them like a cat over its kittens; but a cat that could talk, a cat that could say, 'My baby, my baby,' over and over again. 'My baby, and oh, oh, at my breast, the little hands, the hunger, and that unspeakable agonizing pleasure! Till at last my baby sleeps, my baby sleeps with a bubble of white milk at the corner of his mouth. My little baby sleeps . . .'
>
> Yes . . . you may well shudder.[1]

To complete the picture of our brave new world, the credit crunch is history, our descendants are conditioned to adore shopping and consumption is seen as the bedrock of stability for the World State.

Huxley's prophetic vision articulated a prevailing unease, among those who could at least think, at the way the Industrial Revolution and mass production were bringing about vast changes to the world. Today, across the World State, the number of young children and infants attending daycare centres has risen dramatically and the age at which they first enter daycare centres is younger. And for those with a diploma in childcare, the future's looking blindingly bright. In studying 'the need of non-relative childcare', the US Department of Labor's report Child Day Care Services states:

> Employment in child daycare services is projected to increase rapidly, and an unusually large number of job openings will

result each year . . . Furthermore, growing numbers of parents will hold jobs that require work during weekends, evenings and late nights. As a result, demand will grow significantly for child care programs that can provide care during not only traditional weekday hours, but nontraditional hours as well. In addition, school-aged children, who generally require child care only before and after school, increasingly are being cared for in centers.[2]

Many people point to feminism and a preoccupation with enabling women to compete with men on a completely level playing field in the job market as fuelling this thirst for daycare centres. But liberal–left feminism has become the unwitting bedfellow of naked capitalism – a victim of demographic date rape.

There is a vested interest in playing down differences between men and women and to regard mothers' and fathers' parenting styles as more interchangeable (see Chapter Four). This view also allows for a more 'flexible' labour market, whereby either Mother or Father can go out to work. And if you can get away with paying mothers less, the labour market may also become cheaper. All of this is important to consider when competing with labour forces like China's.

If we are then persuaded that our young children do just as well whether they are in daycare or at home with their parent(s), the labour market becomes even more flexible – and bigger. By eroding first the sex difference between parents, then that between home and institutional rearing, we, as parents, are reduced to flexible labour units that can boost the Gross Domestic Product.

Rising, right along with the number of children going to daycare, is the number of different parenting books being published. A state-of-the-market article in *Publishers Weekly*, entitled 'Parenting by the Books – Lots of Them', talks of customers in terms of 'the time-strapped parent who hasn't the luxury to ponder broad overviews of childcare as in days of old – not when the culture is changing so fast'.[3] The culture has changed, and continues to do so fast and faster still, but we have to ask: have the basic needs of the *child* changed and is this brave new world meeting that child's needs?

Entire economies have a vested interest in the answers to these questions. And to complicate the matter, sexual politics has reared its head again, making the subject incendiary.

The whole affair has been reduced to comfy-speak and the issue has been falsely posed in terms of an ongoing 'debate' with equally valid 'points of view' infantilised with the name 'the Mommy Wars'. But the language is all wrong, as it is concerned with the feelings of the parent, not the wellbeing of the child. The shield of sexism has also been misappropriated to give this so-called debate an emotive political overtone.

Several years ago, I wrote a book proposal that included a number of paragraphs about mothers, daycare, and child wellbeing. Although it was not central to the proposal, I was soon informed that 'the Northern European agents say the women commissioning editors don't want to hear about this subject; it will make them feel angry and guilty. So if you want to get your book published, remove any mention of mothers, daycare and child wellbeing – even if it's true – or else say positive things about mothers, daycare and child wellbeing . . . as they won't be able to make a profit.'

Fortunately for me, my female editor and my female agent (who are both also mothers) are perfectly able and positively enthusiastic about addressing this issue honestly, even if it is uncomfortable. I feel I have to say that none of this is intended to be accusatory or to make mothers feel guilty. The aim is to provide an honest overview of what is going on in the lives of many *children* today, so we can stop and assess things.

This truly is a brave new world for mothers, many of whom are likely to have had a career for a decade or more before having a child: this is history in the making. The variety of experiences and types of stimulation are greater in the life of a single working woman. Humans become attuned to a baseline of daily variety and stimulation and a drop in these can easily lead to a sense of monotony and lack of fulfilment. Long hours spent wiping bottoms and feeding on demand are unlikely to provide the same buzz as a full-on career. So the culture shock that ensues when today's woman's first child arrives is bound to be far more intense than her predecessors' experience ever was. For many women, a career means having some degree of power and influence, and that's certainly reversed at 3 a.m. when their baby's screaming and their left breast has gone dry. In many ways, life goes from 'intellectual' to primitive and instinctual – it seems like a decided step backwards, like going from master to work experience.

Obviously, there are large numbers of mothers who have no choice whatsoever and have to work; in the United States, both parents in many families have been forced to work full-time just to afford healthcare insurance for themselves and their children. And, of course, the recession has turned life upside down for numerous families. But there are many mothers who state that they choose to work (the media often refers to 'those of us mothers who choose to work'); they are not forced to take on all that they do. And, at the same time, governments choose to not support the practice of mothers spending too much time with their own children.

But, perhaps the most inconvenient truth was revealed in Huxley's *Brave New World*, where all men and women are conditioned to consider consumption and economic growth as an assumed norm. When I think of many families with two working parents, I find the man and woman presuming they can, and should, maintain a similar standard of living to that they enjoyed when they were both working and childless. What often follows is a large mortgage, a loft extension, two family holidays abroad, two cars (each no more than three or four years old), evenings out at least once a fortnight, plenty of activities, clubs and lessons for their children – the list goes on and on and requires a double income to satisfy it. To question this presumption, and to suggest that becoming parents involves hefty sacrifice and a drop in living standards, is to question the very basis of our shared values – the foundations of our modern culture. To complement a belief in consumption and growth, society has been sold the tidy idea of daycare, without being fully informed about some of the more problematic aspects that are now coming to light.

The term daycare in this chapter generally refers to a child being cared for in an institution, such as a crèche or nursery, during the first four and a half years of their life. Some researchers, for their studies, define daycare as any care provided by anyone other than the child's mother – including that given by fathers, grandparents and other relatives – that is regularly scheduled for at least ten hours per week. The age at which a child starts (for example, three months versus three years old) and the number of hours a week in question (six versus thirty plus) seem to be related to the problems discussed below. But, generally speaking, the earlier a child starts in daycare, the more changes they experience in daycare arrangements and the more hours per day/week and years they attend, the more pronounced the effects are likely to be. Aside from the increase in children attending daycare centres, many are looked after by foreign au pairs who are very young, inexperienced and speak broken English, but who are inexpensive to hire.

Unfortunately, there is not as yet a recommended daily allowance or dose of daycare, but common sense (which, nowadays, is not considered acceptable in making judgements about our children's wellbeing) should, if we're honest, enable us to decide what is and isn't good for our young children. The main point here is that more and more of our children are having their behaviour and emotions moulded (or not) at younger ages by people who are paid to 'care' for them, but who do not love them. At the same time, we have an enormous problem with the behaviour and emotional make-up of children of all ages, and we have to consider how these early child-rearing experiences may contribute to this. These thoughts may be uncomfortable and may arouse guilt, but they must stop being elevated and therefore almost dismissed as political debates or, on the other hand, merely equally valid lifestyle choices.

The main taboo, particularly if you're a man, is that 'you mustn't make mothers feel guilty'. After all, they are the new sacred cows. However, this discussion is about *child* wellbeing, not about parental guilt, be it maternal or paternal. After all, none of us has any reservation about making fathers feel guilty. Have we become so self-centred that a truthful discussion is too dangerous, even when it involves the best interests of our own children? And, by the way, there has been a substantial group of mothers – stay-at-home mothers – who have been undervalued, and their feelings may be positively enhanced by this discussion. If we are so concerned about sexism and being sensitive to women's feelings about their choices, why must the negative feelings – the guilt – of some working mothers take precedence over boosting the feelings of stay-at-home mothers?

I have tried to review a variety of studies purporting to answer the question: is there any real difference between a biological mother and an institution? But, as with the previous outbreak of mindless openmindedness that still surrounds the question, 'Are men and women really different?' (see Chapter Four), I find the overriding climate inherently corrupt. Again, it seems there's an entire industry unrestrained by common sense. As someone once said: 'The truth belongs to those who commission it.' And stay-at-home parenting and Mother Nature don't have an economic lobby group.

I have read much research, all of which chooses its words somewhat too carefully to be convincing. To claim seriously that babies or toddlers placed in daycare centres for a significant proportion of their developmental years will have just as warm and intimate a relationship with their mothers as those who are not is, quite frankly, insulting to one's intelligence. In short, this means that the many mothers who have spent years at home with their children in the belief that this conferred significant benefits to them have wasted their time. It means that theirs has been nothing more than a discretionary lifestyle choice, a mere stylistic consideration.

There has been an exceedingly unhealthy aversion to discussing whether, and exactly how much, our children need their parents, particularly their mothers. I was warned never to bring this up at any social gathering in Manhattan: it's the unmentionable. When the issue is forced into battle in the Mommy Wars, it focuses upon 'evidence-based outcomes', measured in terms of cognitive ability and personality development. Curiously, it never seems to involve what the experience of daycare actually *feels* like for the infant or child. Ironically, this kind of evaluation can only really be done effectively by the child's own mother, who can read them like a book.

Enter Professor Martha Toadstool-Fink of Bottom's Up Open-Minded University again:

> Thank you so much for your generous donations which helped in the fight to discover whether men and women are really different. Now my research team can turn their attention to an equally unnecessary question – are mothers really necessary and is there a difference between an institution and a Mommy? Does your child really care if you pay an employee who doesn't love them to spend their weekdays with them as opposed to spending those days with you? Research funds can be donated to savethedaycare@mommywars.com . . .

This self-invented debate has, at the very least, lent an air of parity to the position of each side in the Mommy Wars. And this continues to influence important government policies on maternity leave, working mothers and childcare. Most importantly, this academic pantomime is affecting our children and their behaviour towards one another and us.

The one theme that does seem to run through the effects of non-maternal childcare is children developing more aggressive and belligerent, disobedient behaviour when they start school.

While I've read the studies, it is real life that has convinced me that there is a difference in the attitudes, behaviour and empathy of many children who attended daycare centres during key stages of their first four years of life, and I've personally observed this in England, the United States and in that paragon of progressive parenting – Scandinavia. I've noted the differences when we have other children over to play at our house or come for birthday parties. In a number of cases, I've been talking to a parent while their child repeatedly kicks and even punches them as we speak to try and get their undivided attention. I see older children (aged between seven and ten) talk to or sneer at their parents – usually their mother – contemptuously, delivering their remarks with a retrospective resentment. The parents, for their part, seem far more tolerant of being a punch-bag than you'd expect, and I sense that their cultivated forbearance is due to guilt.

Of course, as an outside observer it's easy to pronounce that you can't make up for daycare guilt by accepting bad behaviour, and that parents' guilt and tolerance will backfire on their child's behaviour and on the rest of us.

I was recently speaking to a highly respected headmaster with decades of experience who told me, in hushed tones: 'I can tell those students who experienced delegated parenting; there's something about them, and there are more problems.' He also felt troubled that he was unable to mention this professionally because, 'You're simply not allowed to talk about these things or else you're accused of either sexism or trying to make mothers feel guilty and you could end up losing your job.'

At a more subtle level I, as well as many mothers, have noticed a difference in eye contact with daycare children. They don't seem as able to lock on to your gaze and stick with it for very long, perhaps because they experience less one-to-one parental eye contact on a daily basis and are used to flitting from one child to another or between careworkers.

I must emphasise that I do not offer these observations as a form of academic evidence; they are my own opinions. However, they do also seem to tally with some of the general conclusions of those who have attempted to study the issue formally.

For example, a study published in the journal *Psychological Science* found that just being in a classroom with a high proportion of children who have extensive childcare histories affects those children with little or no early childcare experience. 'So if your child had no childcare, but ended up in a class where lots of children had childcare, your child ends up being more aggressive. There is a contagious effect.' The study also found that children who had been placed in childcare of *any* kind, and for longer hours and at earlier ages, displayed far more problem behaviour. 'If the only way to survive in class is to push and shove, then all the children will think, "Let's push and shove, too."' They're also concerned that as a result, teachers may be less able to manage discipline when there is a high proportion of disobedient children in the class.[4, 5]

And another study reinforces this. Children who spend a lot of time in nursery are more likely to be aggressive and disobedient throughout primary school, no matter how excellent the nursery, it found. These children, even at the age of twelve, are still 'getting into fights' or 'arguing a lot'. It concluded that the 'enduring link between early childcare and child development detected in this inquiry indicated that children with more experience in center settings continued to manifest somewhat more problem behaviors through sixth grade [twelve years old] . . . the effect of center care on externalizing problems remained significant and did not dissipate in strength over time meaning that in the case of nonrelative care, it is center care that has unique and enduring impact of a seemingly adverse kind.'[6] 'Good-quality care simply does not protect against these developmental consequences (like aggression), I am truly sorry to say.'[7]

Fortunately, the authors did not shy away from the social implications of their findings – 'This contemporary situation raises questions about the potential collective consequences across classrooms, schools, communities and society at large of small enduring developmental differences among children who vary in their early child-care experience.'[6] 'Children seem to be spending more and more time and at younger and younger ages in non-maternal care arrangements in the English-speaking world. This means that small effects, when experienced by many children, may have broad-scale consequences.'[8]

For me, it isn't the findings of these studies that is interesting, but the behind-the-scenes political backdrop to the whole issue of childcare research.

A prominent child development researcher, Professor Jay Belsky, Director of the Institute for the Study of Children, Families and Social Issues at Birkbeck University, London, headed a research team that included Harvard University and the National Institute of Child Health and Human Development. In 2001, the team were about to publish their findings that childcare is not good when Belsky's colleagues realised the implications and started acting strangely. Belsky's unofficial insights have been even more illuminating than his empirical ones. He publicly revealed political pressure and the censoring of inconvenient news regarding daycare, even revealing that his own colleagues were 'running from this data like a nuclear bomb went off' because they were committed to showing daycare in a positive light. Belsky said that if his research team's childcare research results had been favourable to daycare, his colleagues would not be seeking further analysis. 'They're so busy trying to protect mothers from feeling guilty, they've lost track of the science. One set of findings gets emblazoned, and the other gets censored.'[9]

An entirely different 'evidence-based' approach to the issue of childcare involves measuring levels of cortisol (the stress hormone) produced by children while they're in daycare as opposed to at home. A review and 'meta-analysis' of nine studies – 'Children's Elevated Cortisol Levels at Daycare' – concludes:

> Our main finding was that at daycare children display higher cortisol levels compared to the home setting. Diurnal patterns revealed significant increases from morning to afternoon, but at daycare only. The effect of daycare attendance on cortisol excretion was especially notable in children younger than thirty-six months. We speculate that children in center daycare show elevated cortisol levels because of their stressful interactions in a group setting.[10]

And the effects appear to be long lasting. A large-scale study in 2009 involving nine institutions found that cortisol levels are abnormal fifteen years after a child attended daycare, regardless of the quality of the childcare facility, the child's gender or ethnicity, the family's income level, the mother's level of education or the sensitivity the parents exhibited towards the children as teenagers. It is thought that these children may be more prone to stress in their teen years.[11]

Academics continue to ponder the 'independent variables' that may influence 'social skills' and other aspects of a child's wellbeing at home versus daycare; however, some obvious explanations are hardly far-fetched. Civilising our children, if I may use this old-fashioned term, requires motivation, attention, observation, time and empathy. And a biological mother has evolution right behind her before the process even starts; she can read her child's emotions and relate them to their behaviour. All of this occurs subconsciously and intuitively, without an NVQ in daycare.

A daycare worker may like a child very, very much but will not have the same emotional attachment to them as their mother. And they will also have to dilute the attention and eye contact they can give between (at least) several other children. Furthermore, given the current political climate, daycare workers (or even teachers) are exceedingly reluctant to sanction a child in the way that their mother can, without even thinking; they don't have the same licence and they certainly don't want to lose their jobs. Plus, they're unwilling to give them the same level of physical affection – if any – for the same reason.

To compound matters, irrespective of what does or doesn't go on at a daycare centre, the separation between child and mother – and sometimes father – leaves the mother, in particular, feeling beholden and reluctant to discipline her child who can then, of course, get away with more. Children may feel an underlying sense of separation and rejection and will push their mother's buttons, and so the cycle continues.

Mommy dearest

In order to have influence over their child, to carry authority and establish boundaries, a parent will be in a much stronger position if they are physically present and put the hours and years in. During the early years, mothers have the potential to have a powerful effect on their child's development and social behaviour, often without having to lift a finger.

Children absorb many things from their mothers in ways they don't from outsiders. Yet political and economic interests have been trying for some time to separate women from their evolutionary history. For example, only a short while ago mothers were told, or allowed to believe, that bottle feeding is as good as breastfeeding. More recently, they were told that so-called 'educational' DVDs such as *Baby Einstein* or *Brainy Baby*, or supposedly 'educational TV', would enhance their children's cognitive and intellectual development.

However, nothing can rival a mother's superior skill in this area and many others. To rub in this important point, a study published in the medical *Journal of Pediatrics* found that the use of these substitutes for a child simply hearing their own mother's voice might actually *retard* their language development, and they showed no positive effects on children aged two and under. One of the authors stated, 'The evidence is mounting that they are of no value and may in fact be harmful.'[12, 13]

France's broadcast authority has just banned French channels from promoting TV shows at all to children under three years old, stating: 'Watching television can slow the development of children under three, even when it involves channels aimed specifically at them.' And few parents are aware that two eminent academics at Harvard Medical School published an essay, 'Say No to *Teletubbies*', or that a study recently presented to the International Communication Association says: 'We would like to think it could work, that *Teletubbies* and other programs can teach initial language skills. That is not true.'[14, 15, 16]

The number of children with speech and language problems has soared by 50 per cent in four years. But these examples aren't only about speech; they're about the power mothers have to shape all kinds of behaviour, including social – i.e. spoilt – behaviour in their children in ways that others can't. A lack of time in the early years can inadvertently detract from a mother's ability to establish authority and sway, which makes setting boundaries and enforcing them more difficult.

A mother's vast superiority in shaping her child's current and future behaviour, spoilt or otherwise, begins early – before they're even born. Newborns prefer hearing their own mother's voice to that of a female stranger, and will even change their behaviour to elicit it. But this 'preference/recognition' begins when they are still in the mother's womb. A foetus can recognise its mother's voice and even distinguish it from others. A study entitled, 'Effects of experience on fetal voice recognition' found that: 'Foetal heart rate increased in response to the mother's voice and decreased in response to the stranger's.' This confirms what scientists have speculated about for decades – that experiences in the womb help to shape later preferences and behaviour in our children.[17, 18] In other words, establishing authority begins down under.

Leaving the womb now, we travel to the other side of the earth and take one step down the evolutionary ladder, where we find that a mother's unique ability to shape her own child remains. Primatologists in Kyoto, Japan, are trying to understand more about how our ancestors learnt and passed on culture and behaviour from one generation to the next. They've spent thirty years observing social learning in the Japanese macaque monkey (also known as the Japanese hot tub monkey because of the amount of time it spends relaxing in naturally heated volcanic hot springs). The primatologists have discovered that when it comes to passing on culture and behaviour, an infant's *proximity* to its mother had a significant impact on the development of, for example, stone-handling abilities. Whether handling stones, emotions or impulses, time with and distance between mother and child matter. Mother or jacuzzi-loving macaque – Mommy can't be outsourced so easily.[19]

Mother superior

Society has been celebrating the liberation of woman from her own evolutionary history instead of her unique, inherent, unrivalled power in advancing her child's wellbeing. And the by-product of these premature celebrations is spoilt behaviour. We should have all along safely assumed that when it comes to socialising children, a mother is superior to any of the pale imitations offered up until proven otherwise. In years to come, these efforts to play down this bald reality will hopefully come to be viewed with shame. And the positive link involving time spent between mother and child and a better socialised child will be acknowledged, if only reluctantly. Motherhood is an incomparable responsibility carried out by a gender with awe-inspiring qualities. Yet our culture bathes the status of motherhood – a timeless role – in mixed messages, and women too feel ambivalent about it.

A woman's ability to conceive peaks at around age twenty, yet most women are now having children far later than previous generations and fewer of them. With this enormous demographic shift has come a powerful change in women's expectations and attitudes towards their children, directly contributing to a spoilt generation. Many women have found it far more difficult to conceive and when they do finally have an only child, the value of that child and tolerance towards their behaviour is understandably different from that of a twenty-two-year-old mother who's between her second and third child. The older working mother with one child is likely to be more accepting of spoilt behaviour, more likely to indulge her child through guilt and will have less energy for confronting her child when they've crossed boundaries and challenged her authority.

Thick and unobservant as I am as a male, I have started to notice the way in which professional women without children view mothers. And there's a general attitude that having a job in an office is more sophisticated and important than looking after your own children as a stay-at-home mother. Perhaps this is why we inevitably hear mothers saying, 'I can't wait to get back to normal life,' implying that rearing children at home is not normal, nor is it as respectable or rewarding.

One of many examples I recall is of a media mother, someone who has a powerful influence on the way parenting issues are broadcast. I was waiting to be interviewed on a television programme and overheard the executive producer discussing a major news article raising questions about mothers who prefer their children to go to daycare centres and focus on a lot more 'me' time. She turned to me and, assuming that I would agree with her lad-like take on the matter, laughed with mild derision, saying, 'What nonsense – life's too short. I have three kids and I drop them off at the daycare centre every day.' Everyone laughed in complete agreement, and it was clear to me that this is the accepted editorial line on professional women, motherhood and childcare. I've heard similar things directly from the mouths of those producers and journalists who influence the nature of public discussion of childcare. This is hardly a good backdrop for a new generation of mothers trying to muster up the pride, motivation and sheer energy to invest themselves fully in the tough job of socialising their children.

The ambient values hovering over society whisper quietly, 'So, stay-at-home mothers are less important'. But the demotion doesn't stop there. Many mothers, to add insult to injury, feel less attractive and less interesting. It seems as though they feel that if they were working again and their children could be in 'high-quality daycare' they would regain control over their lives, along with the esteem that has been missing in their lives. I even get the impression that they think they would actually be slimmer, better made-up, more fragrant and more fashionable.

Ironically, while countless mothers are decrying their utterly thorough lack of appeal, a burgeoning market in wayward websites is making a fortune from their self-hating existence, visited by millions of men each day. Type the word MILF (Mothers I'd Like to Fuck) in to your Google search engine and you'll see over sixty-three million web listings – and rising. Men around the world are at this very moment typing in their credit card details, paying to look at pictures of naked mothers or films of 'Hot Moms Having Sex – Now!!' One of many websites is 'MILF Hunters: Hunting down mature moms across America . . . Hottest Moms in Reality Porn!!!'

If our culture continues to erode the inherent value and status of motherhood, is it not likely that our children will inevitably suffer? If mothers are less fulfilled through motherhood, then ultimately will they not be less able to invest in it? And it follows that if mothers don't invest time, energy and conviction in parenting, authority will suffer, as will the behaviour of our children.

Quality time

In many ways, the term 'quality time' encapsulates the shift of emphasis in the mother–child relationship. We often hear working mothers say, 'Ah, yes, but I spend *quality* time with my children', but have we ever openly questioned what this different time zone actually means? The implication is that there is something better about the smaller amount of time this mother spends with her children. But look more closely and you'll discover that quality time has been defined here entirely by the parent, not by the needs of the child, often being almost scheduled into a busy working week. In reality, 'quality time' is something that can only be defined by the child and often occurs spontaneously: when a child bumps their knee and is comforted by their own mother at that moment; simply enjoying some togetherness by cuddling up on a sofa together; the knowledge that Mummy has made their lunch. In fact, 'quality time' often takes place without the mother even being present in the room; just knowing that she's in the house, even if she's not seen, is a powerfully reassuring feeling for a child. As someone recently said to me: 'A child needs to know that their mother's presence is a spirit in the house.' Real quality time is usually unplanned, undefined and can occur at all times of the working day, as well as the highly inconvenient middle of the night. In fact, in many ways, it's akin to libido and passion – it's a feeling, not an appointment.

Institutional daycare, particularly for younger children and for longer hours, continues to contribute to the creation of spoilt children who needed more contact with their parents, particularly their mothers. And quality time is not a substitute for the sheer *amount* of time children need every day from their parents.

No leave from maternity

Mothers talk about 'going back to work' after maternity leave, but in a sense there is no leave from maternity, as children's needs change in character but not in substance as they get older. More adult company is then needed for gentle guidance, conversation, help with their problems and encouragement. And they have to be monitored from a distance because they are vulnerable to more risks outside the home than ever before, yet they have greater autonomy.

Mothers may have 'moved on', but children haven't. And that needs to be our reference point from now on. If *we* don't see parenting as important, it implies that we don't see children as important, and what will our children make of these values? Will they respect us as parents if we don't value the roles we occupy? How will this affect their self-esteem? And how can we expect them to respect our authority, boundaries and parental decisions?

Our government seems enthusiastic about socially engineering the way we view people whom they consider to be hard done by, for example those with darker skin colour or of lower class. Positive discrimination has been institutionalised quite openly to embrace all kinds of 'diversity'. Curiously, however, one overwhelming area that transcends race and class is the enormous minority of a tribe called mothers. In an ideal world, if our government is so interested in social engineering, why don't they turn their tools towards fighting for stay-at-home motherism? At a practical level, professionalising the role of motherhood requires propaganda and hard cash to enable mothers to be supported financially for doing the most important job of their lives. Any argument that this would detract from the economy and the public purse must be weighed against the social and therefore economic price we pay for a generation of children (and then adults) who are socially unviable. It's called our quality of life and it's certainly worth the investment.

While government PR departments gush terms, such as family-friendly policies, flexi-hours and maternity leave, these often amount to meeting the needs of the parent and the economy, not the child, and are obviously viewed as the 'progressive' reforms of a more civilised society. Civilised for whom, exactly? The child?

Many mothers in Sweden have, after thirty years, asked why they can't look after their own young children, rather than being pressured to allow the government nurseries to do it for them. And there is now a backlash, so that in some areas mothers will be offered a choice either to continue using the state-run childcare facilities or to receive the equivalent money to look after their own children at home. Our government should take note. There have been continued attempts to get mothers of young children, especially single mothers, back to work. This cultural and political imperative should now be reversed. If anything, mothers should be paid to home-rear their own children, or there should be significant tax breaks, and this should take precedence over all other considerations.

At the same time, the phrase 'family-friendly' should be reclaimed. It has been hijacked and distorted to mean: how can we make it as easy as possible to get mothers back into the workplace? What it should really mean, however, is: what working hours and conditions for mothers are best for the children in the family?

Beyond any steps that governments can take, parents everywhere can and *should* be made aware of the difference between sending their child to a daycare centre at the age of six months as opposed to the age of three, and between their three-year-old going to daycare for nine hours a week as opposed to thirty-five. Furthermore, common sense should tell us all that babies and young children need a very low child-to-carer ratio (about one to three). And as with the government's more recent position lauding the superiority of breastfeeding over formula milk, they should take an equally clear stand commending the general superiority of child-rearing from birth to age four and a half by the child's own mother, whether this is what people want to hear or not. These are the very early steps in helping the next generation to develop into a less spoilt one.

Aldous Huxley died in 1963, but it would be interesting to know how close he thought his brave new world had approached today's reality. At the moment, it strikes me that one of the few changes he would make in a new edition would be to change his term 'Conditioning Centre' to 'Daycare Centre'.

Six

Wait Till Your Mother Gets Home!
Absent fathers and spoilt children

For an assortment of reasons (including long working hours), and in a variety of ways, children are being increasingly deprived of paternal parenting. This has direct consequences for their behaviour and wellbeing, and the father's current lack of authority in the family is also a result. Underlying much of this deficit is a failure to acknowledge both the father's unique contribution to child development, as well as the need and right of children to be parented by their father as well as their mother, whether they have separated or not. Sadly, this issue has been consistently portrayed as a group of desperate, unfit fathers fighting for their political rights to see their children, when it should actually be seen as a question of *children's* political rights to see their fathers. Times have changed. The pendulum has swung; man has suffered a reversal of fortune, especially in the family courts. But so have his children.

The following case study has avoided embarrassment to those concerned by almalgamating very similar true cases as one.

14 August 2007, 5.38 p.m.: Graham, an IT consultant, arrives home from work unexpectedly early. He and Fiona have been married for eight years and have two young children, who he adores and is very involved with. As Graham opens the fridge, he notices a piece of paper that has fallen under the door. It's a hotel invoice. He asks Fiona what it is for; her explanation sounds odd. Graham becomes concerned, and when he then discovers an email to Fiona from a man telling her how much he enjoyed their last 'session' – recounted in graphic detail – Graham confronts his wife. (The sessions, by the way, involved the other man slapping Fiona hard across the face, pulling her hair while calling her 'you dirty little whore' and, finally, peeing on her, fortunately in a hotel bathtub.) At first, Fiona denies everything, but after Graham points out the email, Fiona finally admits she is having an affair, regularly meeting her lover in hotel rooms that she pays for (with Graham's income).

Graham – the husband who doesn't slap his wife, pee on her or rebrand her as a 'dirty little whore', apparently much to her chagrin – is distraught. He cries, telling Fiona, 'It isn't even as if we've had any problems or rows, and our sex life is good . . . I love you and you've really hurt me . . . How could you do this?' When Fiona sneers, looks away and refuses to answer, Graham grabs her by the wrist and pulls her to the front door saying, 'Get out! I don't want to see you right now.' He then sits on the sofa with his head in his hands.

But the soap opera is just starting. Within an hour, the police arrive, and, after informing Graham that he is under arrest for 'assault' (grabbing his wife by the wrist), he is hand-cuffed and thrown into a cell overnight. He is told not to return to the family home. Fiona won't let him speak to or see their children, because, of course, he has shown himself capable of 'domestic violence'. She does, however, allow her lover to come over and sleep in the marital bed, as well as spend time with Graham's children ... while Graham, thanks to Britain's 'no-fault' divorce, is required to pay the mortgage along with the council tax, electricity, heating and water bills, ensuring that his replacement can have a warm bath every morning after peeing on his wife.

This case study exemplifies the profound social, emotional and legal changes that have come about in a relatively short space of time. And, while well intentioned, these changes are having unforeseen effects on the wellbeing of the children they were supposed to protect. Moreover, the consequences for our increasingly fatherless society now occupy much of the evening news bulletins.

The UK has the highest incidence of single motherhood in Europe. Now, on both sides of the Atlantic, this comes about more and more by choice. Witness a growing number of books published, including, recently, *Knock Yourself Up: No Man? No Problem! A Tell-All Guide to Becoming a Single Mom*, and accompanying workshops: 'By-choice mom and author Louise Sloan tells women more about an empowering option that's growing in popularity. Louise will give you the lowdown on all the how-tos, like finding a sperm bank, asking a friend to be a donor and doing the actual deed (tip: DO NOT use a turkey baster!). Louise will also address crucial questions like, "Is this fair to the kid?"'

The dad deficit

Fathers are indispensable and of paramount importance as figures of authority; they are particularly good at understanding boundaries and policing them. If we want our children to be well adjusted and socially viable and our society to be more civilised as a result, children need their fathers. Most importantly, children need their fathers to have complete licence to fulfil their roles and exert their authority. Yet our children today are suffering the highest level of fatherlessness in our history. The British government has announced that 'the proportion of children living with one parent more than trebled over the past thirty-five years to 23 per cent in 2007'.[1] The highest rate in Europe.[2] The level in the United States is even higher (27 per cent) and it seems to be a growing worldwide trend in industrialised countries.

There has been mounting concern 'to raise the global profile of fatherlessness and the social catastrophe it is causing in First World countries'.[3] President Barack Obama revealed openly, 'I know the toll it took on me, not having a father in the house. The hole in your heart . . .' While Gordon Brown, not particularly noted for his twinkle-toed enthusiasm, has declared: 'I'm a father and that's what matters most. Nothing matters more than that. Nothing.'[4]

The value of a father

The National Responsible Fatherhood Clearinghouse (NRFC) backs 'efforts to assist States and communities to promote and support Responsible Fatherhood and Healthy Marriage'. Their website (www.fatherhood.gov) says, 'Take Time to be a Dad Today', and they 'encourage fathers to become actively involved in their child's life. The campaign offers significant potential to: promote responsible, caring, and effective parenting; encourage and support healthy marriages and married fatherhood; and reduce the adverse effects of father absence.'[5]

The US Department of Health and Human Services has stated, 'Children who live absent from their biological fathers are, on average, at least two to three times more likely to be poor, to use drugs, to experience educational, health, emotional and behavioural problems, to be victims of child abuse and to engage in criminal behaviour than their peers who live with their married, biological (or adoptive) parents.'

In particular, girls are more likely to become pregnant if they don't live with their fathers. A study, entitled 'Father absence, parental care, and female reproductive development', found that separation or frequent changes increase a daughter's risk of starting their periods early, sexual activity and pregnancy. Girls who experienced their parents' separating between birth and six years old showed twice the rate of early menstruation, more than four times the rate of early sexual intercourse and a two and a half times higher incidence of early pregnancy compared to girls whose families were intact. The longer a daughter lived with both parents, the lower her risk of early reproductive development. Girls who experienced three or more changes in their family make-up exhibited similar risks but were five times more likely to have an early pregnancy. For girls who lived with a stepfather, there was a 'significant association with reproductive development'.[6] Similar results have been found in Britain. 'As in a number of previous studies, an absent father (but not an absent mother) during childhood predicted an earlier age of puberty (i.e. an early menarche). The results confirm that certain psychosocial factors (i.e. father absence; presence of siblings) may affect the timing of sexual maturation in adolescent girls.'[7] If the absence of a biological father is causing the early sexualisation of a daughter, then the need for authority and boundary reinforcement – which the biological father could provide – is more important than ever.

In an international comparative study in 2003, it was found that daughters without their fathers were twice as likely to have sex at a young age and seven times more likely to become pregnant as an adolescent. The scientist made the point: 'More important than the absence of a father are the characteristics of the father and what he did. It's not enough to simply have a cardboard cutout of a father sitting on the couch. What the father does is critical.' And what that father does is carry authority and pregnancy-unfriendly boundaries. Furthermore, that paternal authority is directed at potential boyfriends who will listen to and be frightened of a protective father in a way that they wouldn't in the face of a protective single mother. The study also found that girls who grew up in otherwise socially and economically privileged homes were not protected:

> Father absence was so fundamentally linked to teenage pregnancy that its effects were largely undiminished by such factors as whether girls were rich or poor, black or white, New Zealand Maori or European, co-operative or defiant in temperament, born to adult or teenage mothers, raised in safe or violent neighbourhoods, subjected to few or many stressful life events, reared by supportive or rejecting parents, exposed to functional or dysfunctional marriages, or closely or loosely monitored by parents.[8]

So, the biological consequences of absent fathers leave a girl sexually vulnerable with a void in authority and boundary enforcement. A very unfortunate combination.

Father absence is also linked to children becoming physically spoilt: slovenly and obese. In particular, a father encourages more physical activity in his children. Interestingly, a study in the *Journal of Pediatrics* reported that a father's body mass index (BMI – a measurement of the relative composition of fat and muscle mass in the human body) is directly related to his child's level of activity. In a study of 259 toddlers, more active children were more likely to have a father with a lower BMI than less active ones.[9]

The biological dimension of parenting is highly important in understanding how and why biological fathers exert authority and police boundaries in unrivalled ways. Biological parents are generally more discriminating in their care and affection in favour of their own children. All else being equal, parents will love their own children more than someone else's. In a study, 'Biological and Stepfather Investment in Children': 'The evolutionary theory received substantial support when we compare across families. Consistent with other research, fathers invest less in stepchildren and in non-related children of their partner.'[10]

'Father figures'?

The comfortable vernacular of 'father figures' is an attempt to pretend we've moved on from our primitive, inconvenient roots. Because we are divorcing, separating or having children as lone parents at record levels, we need a vocabulary to accompany these changes – terms that bring parity to the way our children are being raised when compared with families raised by two biological parents in the same house.

It's considered enlightened to see such things as 'equal but different'. Besides, we're told, you can't generalise; it all depends on the individual child and the parent involved – families come in many forms nowadays: 'One Parent Families|Gingerbread believes we can build a fairer society for all families, in which lone parents and their children are not disadvantaged ... We recognise that families come in all shapes and sizes and we believe that the diversity of family life should be celebrated.'[11] While this is positioned to prevent children and lone-parent families, as well as stepfamilies, from being stigmatised, it is ultimately dishonest and unfair to them. All family structures are certainly not in any way equal. Biological fathers are vastly superior to 'father figures'. We wouldn't bandy 'mother figures' about as an acceptable term, as we assume biological mothers are not interchangeable with mother substitutes. Pointing out what is optimal or ideal is not the same as stigmatising and criticising those of us who can't have it. We have few qualms about pointing out optimal diets, exercise and sleep patterns for our children, yet when it comes to politically sensitive aspects of their lifestyle, society tries to either obfuscate or shut down the conversation.

Children raised by their two biological parents living in the same house generally have enormous advantages over those who don't.[12]

Loss of contact

We complacently accept that after parents separate, many fathers have less and less contact with their children. For example, a report by the Office for National Statistics found that over a quarter (28 per cent) of children whose parents separated at least three years ago never have contact with their non-resident parent. Even when there is contact, in a high proportion of cases children do not stay overnight with a non-resident parent.[13]

It's also very important to mention a similar phenomenon occurring between children and their grandparents. For example, around 50,000 Welsh children may be being denied access to their grandparents because of the breakdown of family relationships. After separation or divorce, the child effectively loses one parent and then a further loss is imposed on them by depriving them of a relationship with their grandparents. As a child's world changes abruptly and rapidly, continuity in their life is imperative, and grandparents provide an ambient stability to a family. The word 'parents' is in their title because part of what they do is to parent their grandchildren – nowadays often more than the busy professional parents themselves. (It is estimated that nearly two-thirds of all childcare is now provided by grandparents.)

And when it comes to the creation of a spoilt generation, grandparents are the ideal counterpoint to the excess and tolerance of today. Many come from a generation that had greater self-control and consideration for others, fewer material possessions and a modest sense of entitlement. Reducing our children's contact with this set of additional parents is culturally suicidal. The growing estrangement between our children and their grandparents also means that they may not learn to connect with and, ultimately, respect older people, which is a rising problem in the UK.[14]

Legal obstructions

In most European countries, the law is supposed to be informed by 'sexuality equality' and custody can be awarded to either parent, depending on the best interests of the children. At the same time, there has been a trend over the past two or three decades in favour of women's rights in relation to their children. In the overwhelming majority of cases, the mother gets custody of the children. Even in Germany, where joint custody is the legal norm, 85 per cent of children of divorced or separated parents live with their mother. In France, the proportion is the same. In Italy, mothers get custody in 90 per cent of cases; in Britain, the figure is 93 per cent. Many divorcing fathers do not seek custody. But the state should not presume that. And if a mother decides to move far away, even changing continents with the children, in practice the father has little recourse.

As a result, thousands of children lose access to their fathers, either by the courts or an embittered ex-partner or both, which means, in effect, that they are also being denied an authoritative upbringing. But those extreme cases where ex-partners or courts bar fathers from having any contact with their children – many involving fathers who were prevented from seeing their children for good reason – don't give an accurate understanding of this problem. Court decisions granting children only a handful of visits with their father each month stop any meaningful relationships from developing between them. And many fathers and children suffer because ex-wives repeatedly flout visitation rights, something that remains invisible because the courts tend not to enforce the agreements. Fining or imprisoning a mother for violating a visitation/contact order is, of course, 'not in the best interests of the child' – and the mother knows it. A father must spend a great deal of money and time to even attempt to pursue any flagrant violations, and family court systems are excessively slow and cumbersome, so that unnecessarily long separations occur between children and their fathers, both during and after protracted legal proceedings. Furthermore, mothers can – and often do – make false or exaggerated allegations to gain greater custodial control and reduce contact between father and child.

In fact, I know of cases where the mother was found by the judge to have told the most astounding lies and confessed that she had done so, but I'm not able to give the complete details of these here, as in the UK and Europe even the mother's lies in court are considered 'private' under family law – regardless of whether it has been clearly established that she was guilty of lying in a courtroom. It is indeed a complex system, and one which seems to allow vindictive partners to lie through their teeth with few consequences. Overall, the father's effectiveness is reduced, in that little or no contact with his children allows insufficient time for authority, boundaries and the glue that binds these through a close relationship to develop.

I recently began noting cases of children denied contact that I personally know of. What an eye-opener. In England, the legal system seems intentionally designed to mass-produce children with diminished authority and boundaries in their lives.

A case was reported in 2007 – that of Mark Harris who thought he had a happy marriage:

'I loved the time I spent with my children. Not every father could read their children stories, bath them or take them out for walks in their pram.' But one day, Mark returned home to find his house 'looking as though it had been ransacked'. Almost all the furniture was gone. So, too, were his wife and children, and he had no idea where they were. 'I went to the police. I was beside myself, distraught. They said my wife was in a rented house near by, but that I shouldn't go round until the next day. When I did, she told me she no longer loved me,' he said.

While they were waiting for their divorce to be finalised, Harris's wife was consulting a solicitor, with the intention of having his contact time with his children reduced. 'She said it was confusing for them to see me.' The family court agreed, and contact was reduced to three times a week, then to once a week and finally to once every two weeks. Harris was shocked when he realised he was impotent in the matter. 'I petitioned the judge every time, but there was nothing I could do.'

A year after their separation the couple divorced. Again, Harris made a bid to see his children more frequently and asked the court if they could live with him. His ex-wife retaliated, claiming that seeing their father at all was un-settling for the children. So the court simply banned Harris from having any contact whatsoever with his daughters. 'On my wife's word, the judge simply severed all my rights of access. When I protested, no one listened. How could a court order stop me from being a father?'

Every morning, while he awaited a date to appeal against this judgement in court, Harris would watch his children being driven past his house to school by their mother. He'd wave – unable to say hello, but grateful for their smiles. Then his former wife was granted an injunction stopping him even waving to his children as they passed. 'It was incredible. She said it was harassment, and the court believed her. But I carried on waving. I was damned if I was going to be prevented from waving at my own children. Naively, maybe, I assumed the whole business would be cleared up at the next court hearing.'

But it certainly wasn't, or at least not in the way Harris had hoped. He left that courtroom in handcuffs, sentenced to four months in prison, having been told that waving to his children was tantamount to stalking his former wife. 'On my first night in jail, I shared a cell with a murderer.'

For the next six years, Harris never stopped trying to regain contact with his children. For his efforts, he was rewarded with ten months in prison for contempt of court for driving past his own daughters' house to see them for a split second.

His eldest daughter, Lisa Harris, now reveals: 'One minute, we were normal children; the next, we were in a rented house, with Dad hammering on the door demanding to be allowed to see us. When Dad disappeared out of our lives, we just thought he had stopped loving us. I was certain I'd done something wrong. The first time we saw him waving to us as we went to school, I was thrilled. I remember thinking, He still cares. Every morning, Mum would tell us we shouldn't look at him yet we couldn't help but grin when we saw him. It made our day.'

No one ever explained to Lisa why her father went to prison. 'I was ten years old. As far as I knew, you had to do something pretty awful to go to prison.'

When Lisa was sixteen, she and her fourteen-year-old sister managed to leave their mother, locate their father, pleading to live with him. Now the courts had little alternative but to set aside every previous court order and give him custody. It took ten years and 133 hearings before thirty-three different judges, two prison sentences and a hunger strike before they

were reunited. All of the court hearings and wife's allegations were held in secret and we're not even allowed to know
her name.[15]

While perhaps seeming almost like a soap opera in tone,
this story serves as a lesson in how to diminish effectively the
authority and role of a father in the eyes and hearts of his children. This is precisely why we should be concerned about
fathers having to allocate time, energy and resources towards
fighting contact cases, while having to walk on eggshells so as
not to upset or lose favour with their children, rather than
devoting themselves to the job of being authoritative parents
who can actually socialise their children without needing to
worry about the ramifications. Court cases like these are a
veritable blueprint for fostering the development of spoilt
children.

Pouring poison

In some cases, one parent attempts to influence a child against
the other. This 'parental alienation' is a genuine problem that
goes strongly against a child's best interests. The effect is being
increasingly recognised in the family courts in the UK, often
referred to as 'implacable hostility' caused by the 'controlling'
parent, which is encouraging, but depressing at the same time.

If you want to familiarise yourself with just how much of an
ass the law can be, read on.

In May 2008, *The Times* and other newspapers reported the
case of how a decent and concerned father successfully proved
to the Court of Appeal that his former wife had lied, and for
years poured poison into their daughter's ear in order to prevent contact between them. Senior judge Lord Justice Ward
agreed that the daughter had indeed been influenced by a

'drip, drip, drip of venom' from her mother, who wanted to prevent her from seeing her father. It was utterly clear and accepted by the court that the 'vicious' mother had falsely accused her ex-husband of sexually abusing their child and used this allegation to achieve her aims.

The mother's ploy was so successful that the daughter wrote to her father, when she was only nine, saying that she wished he was dead. ('This is what I really think about you. I hate you . . . You made my life miserable and stressful. I wish you would die.') Lord Justice Ward said: 'The seeds of poison had been sown and from it has grown a wall of dislike, bordering on hatred, for the father.' He described the letter written by the daughter as 'the most ghastly, horrible, letter for a nine-year-old girl to write to her father'.

Lord Justice Ward concluded: 'The mother is, in my view, the source of this state of affairs by corrupting this girl so viciously and turning her against her father.' He went on to say the case was bordering on scandalous, but that the court was compelled to act in the interests of the child, and that because of her mother's 'viciously corrupting' influence, it would now cause their daughter too much distress to spend time with her father. There was now nothing he could do, the judge said, to help the man re-establish contact with his daughter. In a rare show of judicial anger and frustration, he said that decent fathers are left powerless to see their estranged children if vengeful mothers are determined to prevent access. 'The father complains bitterly, passionately, and with every justification, that the law is sterile, impotent and utterly useless. But the question is: what can this court do? The answer is nothing.' In conclusion, Lord Justice Ward said that all he could do was to state that the mother was to blame, and send both her and the daughter a copy of the judgement to read. 'That is the most I can do for you, with a heavy heart. It is a public scandal . . .'[16]

Crime pays.

The Department of Evolutionary and Educational Psychology of the University of Granada has reported that one out of four children involved in a divorce and custody litigation undergoes the so-called parental alienation syndrome (PAS), in which the child is manipulated by the custodial parent, who incessantly tries to arouse in them feelings of hatred and contempt for the other parent. 'This problem is increasingly more frequent.'[17]

More and more, on both sides of the Atlantic, pouring poison is seen by forensic psychiatrists and clinical psychologists as a gross form of child abuse with lifelong consequences for the child on the receiving end. Richard Alan Gardner was clinical professor of child psychiatry at Columbia University from 1963 until his death in 2003. Gardner's life's work was to ensure that society recognised the brutal consequences of this syndrome. His medical paper on PAS, published posthumously in the *American Journal of Forensic Psychiatry*, should be required reading for the spiteful.[18]

In Britain, the *Medico-Legal Journal* published 'Parental Alienation and the Judiciary' to get to grips with the dire, yet hard-to-substantiate, obstacle to children being parented by both of their parents and suffering as a result. The author, Ludwig F. Lowenstein, a consultant psychologist, stated:

> The dilemma is how to deal with the case where the resident partner, i.e. the alienating partner, fails to co-operate with the courts in providing adequate access for the other partner. If the children have been 'brainwashed' and 'programmed' in a particular direction, this made the judge's decision all the more difficult. Many judges have, without always being aware, adopted a double standard. They see mothers who are alienators as 'victims' to be protected even when they have committed what can only be described as a form of 'emotional abuse'. They have abused their powerful position by

influencing the young children and turning them against the other parent. They have usurped the role of the other parent or given it to yet another partner with whom they have become associated. In this way, they have, by destroying the right of the other parent, taken away that parent's opportunity to contribute to the child's welfare. This is at a time when we are seeking to promote the equality of the sexes. Partners should have equal power and responsibility toward their children.

... Judges are often saved by the fact that fathers cease to pursue their role of wishing to play a part in their children's lives. This is due to the resistance they meet from the former spouse, who has often formed a new relationship and wishes the new partner to take over the role of father. I have even known cases where the mother insisted the child call the new husband Dad and the natural father by his first name. Fathers who pursue both their right and their sense of responsibility through the courts are relatively few. Many opt out due to the resistance they meet from their ex-partners, the programmed child and the reluctance of judges to give them justice.

Judges must stop worrying about public outcries if they remove a child from the care of a vicious programming parent, who is showing their hostility toward the former partner. I therefore suggest that the alienated parents, be they fathers or mothers, be protected. In so doing, we are also protecting the children of such a relationship from a gross and calculated misuse of power or position, that of the resident caregiver. [19]

Whether you call it pouring poison or parental alienation syndrome (PAS), the effect is to decimate the influence of one parent, robbing the child of their right to be fully parented and ensuring that the authority, rules and boundaries that might have been in place will not be. But saddest of all, perhaps, is that because a child is made up of both parents, one trashing the other will also damage the child's sense of self.

Deadbeat or heartbroken dads?

We're often led to believe that many fathers do not care about families and children. And the fact that fathers' contact with their children drops or ceases altogether after a divorce or separation supposedly proves the point. However, many fathers have to disengage to save their financial and emotional lives. They don't try to gain sole or even joint custody because they feel, rightly, that the system is stacked against them and that they will go bankrupt trying to fight it.

This whole phenomenon is sometimes referred to as 'ghost dads', fathers who fade away after divorce. But why would a father who loves his children disappear? Why would he hurt them by abandoning them? Aided as they are by the adversarial legal system, divorce, separation, custody and contact are collectively viewed by the father as a win–lose scenario, in which men often feel the loser. A deep sense of shame and failure is created, which men, in particular, do not want to be reminded of. Post-divorce conflicts over child support, parenting and visitation, coupled with spousal criticism, dating, remarriage and job relocation can strain a father's relationship with his family to breaking point. The pain and anger of being repeatedly reminded of what they have lost through circumstances beyond their control drives fathers away, as they choose to avoid, rather than address these emotions, the result being that they 'abandon' their children. In most cases, fathers who stop seeing their children do so for their own self-preservation. This is not written in defence of fathers who stop seeing their children, nor should it be interpreted as such. It is merely an explanation: whether we like it or not, men respond *very* differently to loss and rejection, in this instance exacerbated by the family legal system, and it is yet another politically correct mistake to expect fathers to react like mothers.

Deadbeat or dead dads?

Over the past two decades there has been an alarming global rise in male suicides, with fathers involved in custody and divorce cases featuring prominently in the body count. A variety of studies conducted in North America, Europe and Australia found that one reason may be the discrimination fathers encounter in family courts, especially the denial of access to their children. Fathers facing loss of custody are at above-average risk of suicide.

One researcher who published a major study on suicide in the *Journal of Epidemiology and Community Health* observes that when it comes to divorce and child contact issues: 'Men kill themselves, but women do not ... The courts in the United States are in a position now whereby money is given to the woman, or the man is forced to pay alimony, child support. The man is also asked, in some cases, to vacate the house ... If a man loses custody of the children and the woman keeps those children, there are situations whereby she may not allow the man to see the children, and that causes some depression.'[20]

A report entitled 'Suicide in Australia: A Dying Shame' found that, 'Men were nine times more likely to take their own lives following break-up than women. The difficulty in maintaining access to children also heightens the frustration and isolation of separated and/or divorced men.'[21]

These statistics may seem abstract until you begin to read into them the individual human cost of the current family legal system that is borne by our children. For example, on 13 March 2000, Canadian Darrin White, a father of four, hanged himself in the woods in Northern British Columbia, shortly after being denied access because he could not pay child support that was twice his take-home pay. His fourteen-year-old daughter Ashley wrote a letter to the Canadian prime minister in which she pointed to 'the frustration and hopelessness caused in dealing with Canada's family justice system' as the 'biggest factor' in her father's death. She wrote:

> No one would listen to my father, no one would give him a chance to speak. In this century, everyone hears the woman and not the man . . . He was a kind man who fought a good fight, but no matter what he did or said, he could never win with this system. Things need to change for all fathers going through this same thing. We need to help. Too many kids go without a father because of this. Too many kids are hurt.'[22]

Child Contact Agency?

The British government has announced that fathers are to be more fully recognised: fathers who don't keep up child support payments will be named and shamed on a new website for 'deadbeat dads'. However, they will not be naming or shaming mothers who break the law by refusing to allow children to see their fathers.

In defining 'child support', our society seems to value money paid by the separated father more than it does contact and a relationship between father and child. If there is a Child Support Agency, should there not be a Child *Contact* Agency that values a child's contact with their father and enforces their right and need to see one another if the mother is breaking the law by preventing this? Many fathers pay but can't see.

And, at the same time, mothers may, if they wish, introduce their children to a succession of lovers or boyfriends and step-siblings, while fathers have no influence over this. Should they not be given some say in how quickly a new man can move in with their children after they – the fathers – have been legally required to leave the family home? And should they be given some say in the *number* of new boyfriends that can move in and out during a given period of time? These unmentionable questions demand answers because children are, in the meantime, being exposed to different and conflicting male figures of authority within the home. One father neatly summarises the child–father contact issue: 'Why is it that we talk in terms of fathers "seeing" their kids? If you want fathers to just "see" their kids, they can do that with a photo or video. If you want us to parent our children, then allow fathers to be parents.'[23]

Dadvocates

If you think that child custody and contact is a purely male versus female debate, you're wrong. In fact, some women have been instrumental and, often, far better at fighting for the right of a child to see and be parented by his father. Professor of Educational and Adolescent Psychology Linda Nielsen believes that guaranteeing greater involvement of fathers in children's lives is absolutely vital, and so it is imperative that we 'change laws and policies that don't reflect what the research clearly demonstrates is best for children . . . the fact that both parents are equally vital to the wellbeing of their children'.[24, 25] Nielsen is also President of the American Coalition for Fathers and Children, whose aims seem hardly radical. They simply want children to be able to see and be parented by both parents because of the 'positive effect on the emotional and psychological wellbeing of children'. Her organisation states emphatically: 'We believe BOTH biological parents should be responsible for the emotional and psychological wellbeing of their children, as well as financially responsible. We believe grandparents should have rights and access to their grandchildren.'[26]

Another dadvocate, Professor Marsha Kline Pruett, is educating the legal profession with seminars on 'Fathers Parent Differently than Mothers: Implications for Children and Families Before, During or After Divorce'. She identifies 'the challenges men face in staying involved in their children's lives, maternal gatekeeping, strategies for keeping fathers involved after divorce'.[27]

Others point out that in family courts, the lowered thresholds for the types of conduct that can be construed as violent can be used in child proceedings to make unfounded allegations of violence against fathers on more tenuous grounds than would previously have been acceptable. They believe that allegations of assault should be dealt with by traditional courts, and only actual convictions taken into account in child contact proceedings.

For a child to see their father only every other weekend (for, in other words, about 15 per cent of out-of-school time) is not good. At least one-third of out-of-school time should be the norm in order to enable our children to have a more balanced relationship with both of their parents. This will also give the non-resident parent more authority and greater emotional leeway to parent and deal with boundaries effectively. Children can sense when their father is apprehensive and weakened, when he is treading carefully to avoid confrontation with them, knowing that upsetting them may lead to further contact issues with their mother. With his hands thus tied, a father loses his authority which, in turn, alters his children's behaviour towards him. With his authority eroded, boundaries are crossed with few consequences, as a father on borrowed time is unlikely to want to punish his children. The loss of respect is also reflected in the children's attitude towards their mother, causing a lack of co-operation and discipline all round. This creates the ideal climate in which to produce a generation of spoilt children.

In their Statements on Importance and Implications of Non-resident Fatherhood, the US Department of Health and Human Services believes: 'Contact with one's child has been shown to be necessary for a close relationship ... a close relationship along with authoritative parenting – has often been found to be associated with an increase in children's academic achievement, a decrease in internalising and externalising problem behaviours, and better social and emotional adjustment.' They even go on to say: 'While conflict between parents can exist when a resident father is involved with his child, the positive effect of involvement on child wellbeing outweighs the negative effect of the parental conflict.'[5] Fine words, but in many countries we now need joined-up government which allows this scenario to materialise. In ordinary circumstances, a parent with an established relationship with the child should not have to prove that contact is in the child's best interests. The legal system has to presume that there are ex-husbands, but no ex-fathers.

Children need fathers who have full licence to parent. And there would be more fathers playing a role in their children's lives and fewer ghost or deadbeat dads if they didn't feel so hopelessly defeated by the system.

The children of sexual politics

I have to say that after reviewing the evidence about the crucial role of fathers in our children's lives, accompanied by all the right noises made by our leaders ultimately resulting in inexcusable laws, policies and family circumstances, I'm ordering my Batman suit. Any woman reading this may have more sympathy for children who can't see much of their father and for the fathers' groups who describe this in terms of 'the insidious gender apartheid that separates children from their fathers in the family courts'. Some try to dismiss these complaints as being a veiled misogyny, preferring to view contact with a child in terms of men versus women's rights and wishes. But this is far more important than men's and women's rights – this is parenthood, the self-sacrificial state whereby children are the prism through which our rights must be viewed.

Seven

The Restructured Unit
Stepfamilies

When the powers that be invent interesting terms to describe a social phenomenon, the first thing I do is to ask why? I remember my wheelchair-bound great-aunt reading a leaflet which featured a photograph of a smiley tooth-whitened person with a Zimmer frame, positively beaming about their disability, and which bore the title: *Tips for the Physically Challenged*. 'Physically challenged?' she snorted. 'I'm not "physically challenged", I'm crippled . . . what on earth is the matter with these people?'

When I began to research the way parental authority manifests itself in stepfamilies, my great-aunt's memory loomed large. It seems that the same advertising agency has been retained to rebrand our 'changing family structure'. 'Broken home' was thought to lack something, so we have now seen the emergence of a new term used to describe the stepfamily: 'the blended family'. If one were to be pedantic (and I am), I would point out that in other spheres the term 'blended' denotes an inferior grade, as in blended whisky as opposed to single malt, or blended as opposed to single-estate tea. And it's not clear to me whether the true motives behind this term were to make the adults feel more comfortable or to benefit the children in some way. I also wonder whether it fully acknowledges the feelings of our children.

All the rage

The UK has the second highest proportion of children living in stepfamilies in all of Europe. In the United States, at least a third of all children are likely to live in a stepfamily by the time they're eighteen. And stepfamilies are hardly déclassé: presidents, royal families and role models in all walks of life now cut and paste their family members just like the rest of us. Keeping up appearances isn't what it used to be.

Understandably, we feel that if this is the way we are increasingly living our family lives, we should, at least, try to frame it in a positive way. Few people want to be reminded that their new blended families are usually born of conflict, loss, heart-wrenching change and often conflicting commitments and loyalties. And, frequently, there is an authority vacuum that settles in with the new family – once again, an ideal breeding ground in which spoilt children may grow and flourish.

Just looking at the explosion in the sheer number of relationships that accompany the formation of a stepfamily is illuminating. Our children get tangled in a web of complexity along with our authority. In a family of two biological parents and two children, for example, there are six basic relationships. In a stepfamily of the same size in which each child has a parent from a previous relationship, the number increases to fifteen. And if each of the divorced/separated parents involved has remarried to someone who already has a child from their previous relationship, the number jumps to forty-four. Our two original children would potentially be subject to the authority of six different adults who may well have varying ideas of right and wrong and of what is acceptable or unacceptable behaviour.

There is no 'Waltons' version of a new stepfamily, and forming one will come, inevitably, with more complex problems than in non-stepfamilies. As one observer puts it: 'Raising a family is hard . . . raising a blended family of the same size is about seven times as hard, on average.'[1]

It's usually only in retrospect that people realise that they should, perhaps, have dealt with their stepchildren differently. Being a step-parent is extraordinarily delicate and difficult, particularly when it comes to exerting authority. A veritable Roman arena of family dynamics, reeking of unconscious motives and strategies, administered by Machiavelli himself.

As adults, in love, couples are looking to a brighter future together as one happy family. Strangely, children rarely see it this way. As much as their parents love and look forward, they look back, often in anger and bitterness, and instead of patting their parents on the back and wishing them well, they feel their time may be better spent in dividing and ruling their parents.

Many parents find it hard to credit their small children with the ability to play their parents. But this is, in fact, particularly easy for them to do because, thanks to biology, each parent has a stronger bond with their own children than with their new partner's. This is the thin end of the wedge from which children can start to play the adults in their lives. Adolescents and young teenagers have a longer pre-stepfamily history and are also at a sensitive stage of development involving mood-disturbing hormones – even PMT. Any step-parent trying to exert authority prematurely couldn't have picked a worse child or a worse moment.

Mind the gap

Then, often, there is the child's other biological parent, who is left behind. Children are more likely to adjust successfully to a stepfamily when the non-resident parent continues to see and have a good relationship with them (see Chapter Six), but this is often not the case. Both the biological and the step-parent, understandably, want to avoid clashes with the children while the family is in transition, but this can be at odds with enforcing boundaries and rules – something that often requires confrontation. Children in stepfamilies are more likely to have problems and to act them out, making it more important than ever to spell out, police and enforce rules and boundaries. Children see the void and seize their opportunity. This is particularly difficult for the adult who is trying to avoid coming across as Cinderella's stepmother. They know how important it is to form a warm relationship with the stepchild, yet they also feel expected to fulfil some form of parental role, and the two often seem mutually exclusive.

And there's an entirely different side to this. If there are any custody, visitation or access issues outstanding, parents or step-parents may – rightly – be concerned that doing the right thing and exerting authority, or simply saying 'No', could cause a child to be disappointed and this, in turn, could be used in court against them to justify reduced contact. I've even seen and heard emails and conversations in which the custodial mother has levelled such accusations at a father who was simply performing his duties: 'Zoe told me you made her cry and I'm not so sure she wants to see you this weekend . . . Should I ask her and see what she says?' Ten-second pause. 'She says she doesn't want to come to the phone right now, so I think it's probably best to leave it for the time being.' And it's no coincidence that with the rise of absent parents has come an increase in material gifts to curry favour and assuage feelings of inadequacy on the part of said absent parent, who is usually the father.

And we mustn't forget the possibility that either biological parent may actively seek to undermine the other's authority and that of their new partner. Either way, it's a case of mind the gap, because once children see a crack, they may use it to great effect.

The rules of cut-and-paste

Children in stepfamilies are more likely to be bullies or the victims of bullying and they've learnt some of this from their parents. The conflict they have lived with, and which may still continue with ex- and, perhaps, even new partners, provides them with an in-house learning facility. At a basic level, a child learns that the person with the most aggressive power dominates and carries influence and that others can be hurt in the process. If one child is afforded greater status or influence in the new stepfamily, they will be unlikely to look a gift horse in the mouth and will indulge it to great effect and without pity. And it isn't merely a case of that child being at the top of a pecking order without having to jostle for position, their heels may also be stamping on top of their parents' heads, who may become subordinate. Take, for example, a thirteen-year-old boy who manipulates and dominates both parents: the biological father feels ambivalent about laying down the law, while the stepmother treads carefully to avoid confrontation and to be supportive of the father's position. Her younger son, meanwhile, resides at the low-rent end of the hierarchy, and has learnt to adopt a policy of habitual appeasement and deference to the thirteen-year-old Hitler youth.

Pecking orders in traditional families can leave more than enough scar tissue, but adding non-biological siblings to the mix can easily create far more disorder and a lifetime's painful baggage that shapes or misshapes the personalities of victims and perpetrators.

There is no fine science to establishing a harmonious stepfamily. However, there seem to be several themes that the cut-and-paste experts continually refer to when recommending the ideal recipe for a blended family. Establishing a formidable defence or even a pre-emptive strike against a divide-and-rule strategy by children can shore up authority no end. And while most of society is busy extolling the virtues of transparency, openness and communication, establishing authority and a set of rules in a new stepfamily requires a marvellous blend of secrecy and censorship. The parents' war cabinet should meet and legislate *in camera*. While evidence may be taken from all the children, the parents' authority must be seen to be unanimous and overriding, any mutiny being met with a united front, even if there is disagreement between the parents. Allowing gaps to appear will invite the inevitable.

Where possible, boundaries and rules should be set that appear to apply equally to all children. Obviously, age, sex and other factors will influence the feasibility of absolute equality for all, but a sort of pyramid approach can work well: a basic and general constitution with a more specific bill of rights, dependent on the individual circumstances of the children, which is finely crafted through the use of by-laws to be applied as the parents see fit. Partners should *never* contradict or undermine each other in the presence of any of their children. If there's good reason to adjust the rules, this should be done behind closed doors.

Ex-cess baggage

Ex-partners will often disagree. Curiously, that's usually why they became ex-partners to begin with. Yet some people are surprised to find that their ex-partner does things in a different way from them – parenting, for example. If they couldn't agree on things when they were together, why on earth would it be any easier once they're not? However, as is the case with the united front that's necessary with a new partner towards the children, it's important to establish a second united front with an ex-partner. Children are likely to be scouring the surface of their parents' relationships for chinks and gaps, and it can be harmful for them to see that they disagree too much.

Sometimes, it's a case of agreeing to disagree, in which case both partners must make it clear to their children that there are differences in rules and boundaries in each of the two homes, and that they have agreed to these terms and expect the children to stick to them. Children learn over time that they do things one way in their father's house, and another in their mother's. And by each of the ex-partners agreeing to support the authority of the other for the sake of their children, they can pre-empt divisions and the painful price that is paid for them.

As one parent puts it: 'If you succeed, it means both of you love the child more than you hate each other. If you fail . . . it's normal.'[1] In the case of an insolvable war of attrition between separated parents, both parties need to accept that they can only control their own territory, and that they can't change the other's behaviour. Torturing themselves over their contrary positioning at every turn is a waste of time.

Our house is a very, very, very fine house

Parents should not worry that by setting stricter rules and limits and disciplining their children that they will not like them or their home because it doesn't taste as good as the more easy-going option on offer at the other parent's branch. Again, this is a fundamental and endemic problem based upon a profound misconception that limits are limiting and discipline is damaging, while in fact limits, boundaries and discipline make children feel safe and secure.

Children are unlikely to appear happy when a consequence is imposed, but setting and policing limits and boundaries teaches them, ultimately, that we are doing it precisely because they *matter* to us, because they are loved. Any concerns over the effects of a regime are easily counteracted by having fun together as a family through new family routines: pancakes on Sunday mornings, going to the park on Saturday afternoons or simply playing together or drawing silly pictures. This is the glue that connects the new members of a family. These are the patterns that provide a rhythmic grounding, bolstering feelings of security and fostering better behaviour.

Eight

The Three-parent Family
How electronic media defy parenting

'The television is almost like a member of the family in its own right,' according to both the Broadcasting Standards Commission and the Independent Television Commission.[1] Consider that electronic media now claim more hours, days and years of your child's eye contact and attention than you, their parents, do. Baby DVDs, TV, PlayStations, iPod videos, YouTube and social networking are displacing the vital influence of us parents and other key figures in our children's lives . . . often replacing it with something that is very much at odds with effective parenting. And this unrecognised parent in our children's lives is making a decisive contribution to the creation of a spoilt generation.

Of course, it's convenient for us to believe that free thinking prevails and that we're not that influenced by what we see on the screen. If that were the case, however, the advertising industry would not exist and censorship would be deemed unnecessary by the powers that be. Even those of us who think that being well informed is good for the mind are easy prey for subliminal effects. Just fifteen minutes of a random news programme, for example, can influence your mind: 'Watching the news on television triggers persisting negative psychological feelings: state anxiety, total mood disturbance increase,' according to the study, 'Negative Psychological Effects of Watching the News in the Television: Relaxation or Another Intervention May Be Needed to Buffer Them!'. Furthermore, these feelings could not be buffered by any kind of distraction.[2]

Those of us who think that they themselves are relatively immune to the power of the screen should, at least, acknowledge that children and young people are far more easily influenced by the information they receive because their life experience and critical faculties are not fully developed.

More quality time?

Children today are watching more television and at younger ages than ever before. The average six-year-old in Britain or the US will have already watched television for more than one full year of their lives. When other screen time is included, the figure is far higher. British children aged eleven to fifteen now spend 55 per cent of their waking lives – that's seven and a half hours a day – in front of a screen.[3] Over the course of childhood, children spend more time watching TV than they do in school.[4] More than half of all three-year-olds now have a TV set in their bedrooms.[5] At least two thirds of young British children watch television before they go to school and even more watch when they return home. Twenty-five per cent of British five-year-olds have a computer or laptop of their own.[6] In the United States, by three months of age, 40 per cent of infants are regular viewers of television, DVDs or videos, and by the age of two this number increases dramatically to 90 per cent.[7] A study by the Children's Society found that television is displacing our parental role, eclipsing 'by a factor of five or ten the time parents spend actively engaging with children'.[8]

As was the case with research into sex differences and day-care, many of us are left with the impression that the effects of screen media on our children are still very unclear. However, this is largely because we receive our information from newspapers and television and the Internet, all of which have financial interests in screen media. Even government is doing financial deals with the major broadband providers. Many newspapers own enormous television networks, and even liberal left newspapers receive a lot of advertising from the screen-media industry and are read by those whose livelihoods depend upon making screen entertainment.

Within the last month, for example, while I have been writing this book, two major medical review papers have been published by highly respected paediatric specialists in high-echelon institutions, finding, quite clearly, that television is directly linked with medical and behavioural problems in children.[9, 10] But you never read about it in your newspaper, did you? And most of us are probably far better informed about the Beckhams' joint six-packs, which get plenty of front-page coverage.

Screen entertainment is increasingly linked with not-so-very-nice behaviour and attitudes, ranging from belligerence to a caustic disposition, bitchiness, searing entitlement, a demand for instant gratification, as well as, of course, plain old murder. Aside from the extreme examples of copycat violence, violent video games have direct everyday implications in homes and schools for parents and teachers. An empirical review of the last twenty years' research into the effects of video games presented to the American Psychological Association in Washington, DC, reported that children who played more violent video games had more arguments with authority figures.[11] This may not seem sexy enough to appear in the news, but it is having an enormous insidious effect because it can't be counted in the way that murders and stabbings can. (By the way, British ten-year-old boys spend an average of more than three hours a day playing computer games,[12] many of them violent.)

What underlies this influence is the erosion of a child's ability to control their impulses. This happens partly because screen media displace vital social and emotional development time, and partly as a direct result of the content of the games or programmes in which children are immersed. It is a far more sophisticated effect than the arguments surrounding copycat behaviour might suggest. In fact, spoilt behaviour can, in part, be described as a neurological phenomenon – an alteration in our children's brain development. Watching television is thought to subdue the involvement of the most highly developed part of our brain – the frontal lobe. This is the brain's executive control system, responsible for planning, organising and sequencing behaviour for self-control, moral judgement and attention. Television, like hypnosis, reduces our ability to analyse critically what we are being told or what we see. For example, adding single-digit numbers involves areas throughout the left and right frontal lobes. Watching a television screen does not. Given that adding single-digit numbers is a very mundane task that doesn't require much of your brain, and that television uses even less of it, imagine how much less of the brain is being used when watching television than during more complex activities such as social interaction with our peers – that is, living.

Most worrying of all is that the frontal lobe, which continues to develop until the age of about twenty, may be damaged by watching a lot of television. It is imperative that children and young adults do things which thicken the fibres connecting neurons in this part of the brain, and the more a person is stimulated, the more the fibres will thicken. Doing simple arithmetic or reading out loud, for example, are very effective in activating the frontal lobe. Television, on the other hand, may literally disengage this brain area and stunt its development.

The frontal lobe also has an important role to play in keeping an individual's behaviour in check. Whenever you use self-control to refrain from lashing out or doing something you shouldn't, the frontal lobe is hard at work. Children often do things they shouldn't because their frontal lobes are under-developed. A study reported by the World Federation of Neurology expresses great concern over the way visual electronic media are affecting children, by '. . . halting the process of frontal-lobe development and affecting their ability to control potentially antisocial elements of their behaviour . . . the implications are very serious . . . children should also be encouraged to play outside with other children, interact and communicate with others as much as possible'. The more work done to thicken the fibres connecting the neurons in this part of the brain, the better the child's ability will be to control their behaviour.[13]

The late George Gerbner, a professor of communications who spent a lifetime studying the effects of television, commented: 'For the first time in human history, most of the stories are told to most of the children not by their parents, their school or their church, but by a group of distant corporations that have something to sell. This unprecedented condition has a profound effect on the way we are socialized . . .'[14] The behaviour and values promoted by electronic media have not only displaced those stories with which children would have been enculturated through their families, schools or churches, they have actively replaced them with their own version of child-rearing, often at odds with what we as parents and society want.

Electronic media harness and amplify our children's developing tendencies and desires. In Freudian terms, modern, compelling media stimulate our child's id, the department of instant gratification and pleasure-seeking impulses and basement of the three-tier structure of our personality. But, in doing so, they turn their inclinations into expectations and distort their development. Electronic media give permission to the id. This, however, is a role that should be performed by the child's ego (the rational, reasoning level) and the superego (the conscience) after timely and considered moral and ethical development within a social and parental context. So through default, the development of the child's superego has been unknowingly outsourced to the values of what they see on the screen(s), the new electronic conscience.

Put simply, if we don't rear our children, someone else on a small screen will. And it's unlikely to be our idea of a positive role model. Many parents who would be outraged at the thought of a stranger communicating with their children seem unaware of the stark reality that a variety of strangers may be doing just that, uncensored and for hours on end in their bedrooms.

Looking at the brains of non-aggressive adolescents versus those who have been diagnosed as having disruptive behavioural disorders (DBD), as they watched moderately violent scenes on a screen, provides further clues as to how media may fundamentally change civilised behaviour. Unlike the non-aggressive adolescents, those with DBD showed less brain activity in their frontal lobe, which, as we have seen, is responsible for decision-making, behaviour and impulse control, attention and a variety of other executive functions. What is most telling is that the way in which the 'normal' adolescents' brains reacted to this new televised material is related to the amount of violent media they had watched in the past – in other words, there is a cumulative effect. A follow-up study found that screen violence changed the frontal-lobe brain function of 'normal adolescents' who were previously well behaved, to the brain patterns of aggressive children with DBD: 'media violence exposure may be associated with alterations in brain functioning whether or not trait aggression is present'.[15] These neurological changes have direct implications for children and young people and their challenge to authority.

Empathy

The Internet too may be changing the way in which our children's brains work, making them less aware and concerned with the effect they have on other people, and less able to relate in a civilised way to others. Although the media often crows about Internet and computer use increasing people's ability to make snap decisions and filter large amounts of information, new research is finding that this may come at the cost of the social and emotional skills central to civilised behaviour. In particular, there seems to be a decrement in the subtle skills of reading the nuances of facial expression. When using the Internet, the areas of the brain associated with empathy showed virtually no increase in stimulation. 'Young people are growing up immersed in this technology and their brains are more malleable, more plastic and changing than with older brains ... As the brain evolves and shifts its focus towards new technological skills, it drifts away from fundamental social skills.'[16]

Displacement

While the examples described above relate to how electronic media contribute directly to a spoilt and impulsive generation, an equally important question is what under-recognised things are being *displaced* by the time spent with electronic media?

I've just written a paper on how the increasing use of electronic media has more than 'coincided' with a dramatic fall in eye-to-eye contact and face-to-face social interaction. The paper includes a graph that charts, in hours per day, the amount of time we have spent socially interacting face to face over the past twenty years. In the same graph, a second line charts the amount of time spent using electronic media. It is quite a sobering vision to see the two lines crossing around the year 2000, when virtual life took over from the real thing in terms of how we spend our time. And this crossover has had huge implications for shaping our children's behaviour and the development of their minds, their souls.[17]

This profound change in the way our children are being

socialised is brought into sharp relief again and again when I find myself in foreign cultures in which few or no electronic media are available. The most notable difference is the amount of time that they spend looking at one another and at their parents eye to eye. They also converse a lot more face to face. And when they're not interacting, they are all busy observing other people for hours a day. In rural Kompong Phhluk, Cambodia, where there is no electricity and, therefore, no electronic entertainment for children, I saw them interact, quite literally, face to face for many hours a day. And they suffered no boredom.

On a trip in 2007 to North Korea (a place that feels a little like it's stuck in the 1970s, in that young people have no computers, mobile phones or iPods, but live in buildings with running water and electricity), I witnessed a great deal of face-to-face social interaction. In one memorable instance, I was walking along a path leading to Liberation Tower in Moranbong Park, Pyongyang, when I heard noises in the woods. I peered through the bushes and saw a group of Communist teenage boys, with not a single electronic device between them, putting on little sketches to impress the girls, who then did the same in return. There was plenty of laughing and, I gather, a degree of courtship and wooing going on. But what I noted, above all, was the eye contact, and the fact that these young people were reading, gauging and making judgements based on others' behaviours and reactions.

Children must learn to read, understand and negotiate with other people, and this can only happen if they spend time face to face with other people. There is no virtual substitute. When you look at the reduction in face-to-face family interaction, this issue becomes crystal clear. For example, Britain has the lowest proportion of children in all of Europe who eat with their parents at the table,[18] and 75 per cent of dinners are eaten in front of the television.[19] The Association of School and College Leaders has cited the decline of the family meal as the reason why overstretched schools are now having to teach basic manners to children, as well as how to hold simple conversations. Youngsters too often lack key social skills, such as listening to others, saying 'Please' and 'Thank you' and taking turns.[20]

A new generation of research is finding that, for example, eating meals together at the table confers benefits such as closer families and better-behaved children and young people who learn about interaction through taking part at the table. Eating in bigger, inclusive groups integrates young people, teaching them how to function as part of a group. Antiquated as they may now seem, practices such as saying ritual grace – a 'stilling' – before eating, serving others first and waiting until others are finished before leaving the table, impart deferred gratification, consideration and respect for others. Ensuring our children eat with us at the table is probably our greatest opportunity to socialise them, providing a forum in which our children and young people are made socially viable, and a place where we may impart our values and (hopefully) they absorb them.

Mirroring behaviour

Eating together involves a form of mentoring that goes beyond just learning table manners. Almost as a captive audience who happens to be hungry, children and young people learn through observation and/or copying the 'right things' at the table. In fact, neuroscientists now believe they've identified specialised brain cells called 'mirror neurons', which, when activated, literally make children and young people absorb, mimic and integrate social behaviours. They're also thought to underlie our children's ability to 'adopt another's point of view'. A child's brain is likely to have multiple mirror neuron systems that specialise in carrying out and understanding not just the actions of others, but their intentions – the social meaning of their behaviour and their emotions.[21, 22]

People who rank high on a scale measuring empathy have particularly active mirror neuron systems. A study of the brain activity of ten-year-olds who observed and imitated emotional expressions and social skills found a direct relationship between the level of activity in the children's mirror neuron systems and 'two distinct indicators of social functioning in typically developing children': empathy and social skills. In the journal *Neuroimage*, scientists report that the importance of observing and copying everyday social behaviours and the mirror neuron system 'may indeed be relevant to social functioning in everyday life during typical human development'.[23] It's not surprising, then, that these brain cells have acquired nicknames such as 'empathy' or 'Dalai Lama' neurons. Mirror neurons, by the way, work best in real life, when people are face to face; virtual reality and videos are shadowy substitutes.

Learning to read emotions

Children need to learn how to take part in a conversation in a civilised way by spending a lot of time watching their positive role models do it and being able to take part themselves. In fact, this is quite a technical process and one that is being studied carefully.

New research is going 'against the popular theory that the facial expressions of basic emotions can be universally recognised. A person's cultural experience of others plays a very strong role in determining how they will perceive emotions.'[24] Children and young people need to *learn* this from repeatedly experiencing face-to-face conversations especially within their own family. This is more likely to ensure that they become emotionally literate and able to interpret, even manipulate, others, as required, outside of the family as well as in. Children will not acquire these skills through staring at a screen.

Linguistic and expressive skills

Real face-to-face conversations confer linguistic skills along with the ability to have conversations – to know when and how to listen and contribute. Researchers studying the 'psychological and social dynamics of topic performance in family dinnertime conversation' have found that a variety of vital processes are exercised through face-to-face group conversation: 'interactional and psychological dynamics involved in introducing, sustaining, reintroducing, shifting, discontinuing and ending a topic, as well as the underlying factors that govern topic dynamics during family dinnertime conversations'. The technical-sounding nature of the studies gives us an idea of how complex table talk really is, and what the processes are that are learnt and reinforced during what, to most of us, seems idle chit-chat. The technical analyses continue, explaining that 'participants seem to use certain explicit cues, such as the introduction of new locative, temporal and participant co-ordinates, and implicit cues such as speakers assuming that the conversational participants have the background or frame of reference to interpret what has been said'. Interestingly, 'power-relations' and gender roles in the structure of families are central to 'organising topic development during dinnertime conversation'.[25]

Eating together and mental health

And there are other reasons why non-virtual face-to-face time between family members produces biological changes that translate into better relationships and better behaviour in our children.

A study at Columbia University reports that having at least one parent eat dinner with their child regularly was found to prevent depression, anxiety and substance abuse in children, who also achieve higher grades in school, compared to those children who dine on their own.[26]

Eating together has been held responsible for strengthening marital relationships and children's 'self-esteem'.[27] Children in families who eat together fewer than three times per week reported higher levels of family tension, less conversation and lower self-esteem than families who eat together more often, without television.[28]

Research at the National Center on Addiction and Substance Abuse at Columbia University 'consistently finds that the more often children eat dinner with their families, the less likely they are to smoke, drink or use drugs'. The centre has established 'Family Day – a Day to Eat Dinner with Your Children; eating dinner frequently with your children and teens reduces their risk of substance abuse'. The Chairman of the National Center has even gone so far as to state: 'One of the simplest and most effective ways for parents to be engaged in their teens' lives is by having frequent family dinners . . . one factor that does more to reduce teens' substance abuse risk than almost any other is parental engagement.'[29] And the US Congress now recognises National Family Month (mid-May to mid-June), strongly promoting 'frequent family meals' as the way 'to help America's families reconnect'.[30]

A new five-year study of 2516 adolescents by epidemiologists and consultants in adolescent medicine has found that eating together is so important it should now be considered a health issue: 'Healthcare professionals have an important role to play in reinforcing the benefits of family meals . . . Schools and community organisations should also be encouraged to make it easier for families to have shared mealtimes on a regular basis.' The study found, for example, that adolescent girls who frequently eat meals with their families are less likely to use diet pills, laxatives or other extreme measures to control their weight five years later. 'Even after adjusting for sociodemographic characteristics, body mass index, family connectedness, parental encouragement to diet, and extreme weight control behaviours.'[31]

Before I continue to cite further studies, I should make it clear that eating together is actually a form of intensive parenting, merely operating under the guise of eating. Parents are exerting a powerful subliminal influence through uncontrived role-modelling.

This is precisely the opposite of what electronic media does. In fact, this is why I feel that these studies on family eating are so important: they provide an excellent point of comparison and make us think about the time and influence electronic media are having over the socialisation of our children.

Restoring parental authority over food consumption

Eating together as a family during adolescence is also thought to have lasting positive effects on the quality of our children's diets later in life.[32] One aspect of the spoilt generation is their unprecedented level of body fat. Parental control and influence over how, when and what our children eat has been literally disrupted, making it a major factor in childhood obesity. Eating in front of the television lowers metabolism, with fewer calories burnt than when people are eating together and interacting. There is actually a significant dose–response relationship in which calorie-burning resting metabolic rate decreases as a person's average weekly hours of TV viewing increase.[33] Other research finds that eating with the television on makes both children and adults eat significantly more – the equivalent of one full extra meal a day, even if they are not physically hungry.[34] One of the mechanisms by which television may induce children to eat more works by causing their brains to monitor external non-food cues – the television screen – as opposed to internal food cues that tell them that they are full and can stop eating (or a parent who simply says, 'No, you've had enough'). Experiments have found that when distracted in this way, humans continue to salivate unnaturally in response to more and more food when normally they wouldn't.[35] A study, 'Television watching increases motivated responding for food and energy intake in children', concluded: 'Television watching can dishabituate eating or disrupt the development of habituation [satiation].'[36] Also, screen images of food make children more acquisitive – they want, crave and are more likely to expect, demand or take more food. We shouldn't be surprised; after all, those slow, enticing food adverts work on us too. But who's in charge of food intake here? Sitting down to a family meal reduces the risk of obesity partly because parents, not a TV screen, are in greater control of their children's food intake.[37]

The hormone of affiliation

'It's said that the eyes are the window to the soul . . . they certainly are the window to the emotional brain,' according to the authors of a new study at the University of California, San Diego School of Medicine. 'We know that the eye-to-eye communication – which is affected by oxytocin – is critical to intimate emotional communication for all kind of emotions – love, fear, trust, anxiety.'[38]

Real eye-to-eye contact is being found to alter brain function in both babies and adults. One route is through the release of the 'hormone of affiliation' oxytocin, which is released in the bloodstream in response to everyday aspects of our social interaction including hugging, touch and warm temperature, and is also involved in feelings of trust and generosity.[39] Any parent who is interested in having a closer relationship with their children should be aware that oxytocin is strongly implicated in the bonding between mother and infant, as well as between parents, and even in the increased involvement of the father with his children and with monogamy. Sadly, you can't buy it on eBay.

But going back to socialising our children through good old-fashioned eye-to-eye contact and conversation, oxytocin appears to change the brain signals involved in interpreting facial expressions, perhaps by changing the function of the amygdala (the part of the brain that plays a primary role in the processing of important emotions). Oxytocin seems to play an important role in establishing our children's social behaviour.

The freedom of censorship

A fundamental difference between a child and an adult is that children are more susceptible to the effects of everything from sunburn and alcohol to ideas and images. And while free speech may seem a laudable aim between adults, the concept is now being used primarily by commercial interests to allow them to speak freely to our children. It all sounds very open and honest, but what our children *need* is more censorship.

Children today have a preponderance of ideas, opinions, values and, most importantly, images delivered as a takeaway directly to their eyes and ears, without the knowledge and mediation of their parents. There have never been so many influences 'speaking' freely to our children out of our earshot. Such an imbalance has profound and worrying consequences for parenting and for teachers.

As the information highway becomes wider, and our children become digital surfers, our society's misplaced concern seems to be protecting children from so-called inappropriate content and, of course, online paedophiles. But the main risk for children is insidious and has to do with nudging them in directions that are often at odds with our values and what is good for them. The plethora of adverts alone or even mere images of consumer goods has created the most demanding, acquisitive, materialistic and entitled generation we have ever seen.

But there are the overlooked effects of our children investing so much time in the virtual as opposed to the real world. A study published in Proceedings of the National Academy of Sciences

(2009) examined the brain function and development which underlie abstract qualities such as compassion and morality. The scientists drew specific attention to the effects of electronic media in altering a child's moral compass: 'The rapidity and parallel processing of attention requiring information, which hallmark the digital age, might reduce the frequency of full experience of such emotions, with potentially negative consequences.'[40] One of the authors explained the possible interference with this process by the speed of today's media, irrespective of the quality: 'For some kinds of thought, especially moral decision-making about other people's social and psychological situations, we need to allow for adequate time and reflection. If things are happening too fast, you may not ever fully experience emotions about other people's psychological states and that would have implications for your morality.'[41]

The term 'social networking' rolls off the tongue without much thought. Yet for developing children, it defies the very definition of social. Those drawn to interacting with others through a screen would once have been called introverted or shy. Now, chat rooms are hailed for giving them a voice, and even the more gregarious are spending more time alone. The damage done by displacing key periods of emotional and social development with time in front of a screen doesn't have the sense of dramatic risk that Internet paedophilia does. However, increasing time spent in a virtual world displaces vital development time spent experiencing real socialising, learning to interpret, respond to and cope with the nuances of real emotion, relationships, disappointments and disagreement – the human condition.

Protecting children online is, yes, partly a technical and legal issue involving broadband and browser filters, but at its heart, it is really a parenting issue. If we really want to protect our children, we have to do what parents have always done: mediate and filter what they see and hear within reason. It's funny how we wouldn't dream of putting a refrigerator chock-full of ice cream and fizzy drinks in our children's bedrooms because we know that they'd just help themselves to anything they want – yet more than a third of children have their own computer, and at least one in five can access the Internet privately in their own room.[42] Like fridges, online computers should be within parents' sight and earshot and not in children's bedrooms. It's called real-time censorship and it's the most effective thing ever invented. The main obstacle is a generation of parents afraid of confrontation and of being authoritarian – or, perhaps, too busy surfing themselves to notice.

Nine

Spoilt for Choice

How cultivated deprivation
enriches our children

We normally associate the term 'spoilt' with material over-indulgence, and while this is obviously true in most Western industrialised societies, in many ways this is the least of our worries. The concept of spoilt has developed apace in many spheres of a child's life. But there is one dimension that has made everyone's life more difficult, and, for adults, more complex: the tyranny of options available to us in almost every area of our lives today. We are encouraged to believe that choice and options are the terms of endearment to a democracy: a sea of options gives us autonomy and helps us to shape our lives. Of course, many of us have come to realise that we can easily drown in a sea of options, and that when you think about it, less is usually more. Our consumer society obviously runs contrary to this – but we are adults.

I recently read an interesting academic paper on the effects of choice that I think successfully overturns the assumption that it is necessarily a good thing. The researchers at Columbia and Stanford University threw up their hands in conclusion, asking: 'How can there be so much dissatisfaction in the face of so much opportunity?' And, they posit: 'A standard assumption underlying research on choice is that the provision of a choice will typically increase feelings of perceived control . . . perhaps as the amount of freedom people have increases past some easily manageable bound, people experience an increasing loss of control.'[1] One hundred and eighty years ago, the highly influential French historian Alexis de Tocqueville looked at choice-ridden Americans with bewilderment: 'In America I have seen the freest and best educated of men in circumstances the happiest to be found in the world; yet it seemed to me that a cloud habitually hung on their brow, and they seemed serious and almost sad even in their pleasures.'[2]

It's not surprising that choice has now become the wiggle room that children and young people take for granted, or, perhaps more accurately, simply feel entitled to in almost every sphere of their lives – from their breakfast cereal to where they hold their birthday parties. Part of this is a result of direct advertising, which dangles an ongoing multitude of possibilities in front of their eyes, but it is also partly our failure to limit the choices available and to enforce these limits with conviction. Ignorance is bliss; in other words, what the eyes don't see the mouth is less likely to demand.

The choices made available to our children are often not consumer choices but choices in areas of authority or between courses of action. My local florist recently told me how a child grabbed a bunch of flowers without asking, and when she said to the boy, 'What do you say when you want something?' his mother replied very innocently, 'Oh, Josh doesn't say please, do you, Josh?' looking to her son for his consensus. The florist could only pray for an oversized venus flytrap to re-educate Josh and his mother on the spot.

It's my prerogative

For all its appeal, choice is a double-edged sword, and at the moment, children are feeling the rough side of the blade. Even in a medical context, choice is being found to be detrimental. For example, in the smorgasbord effect, it's easily seen that with more food choices, people eat a lot more: variety leads to greater consumption and ongoing variety leads to higher expectations of consumption. In identifying the causes of obesity in children, the South African Nutrition Expert Panel recently concluded: 'This seems to be a function of too much discretionary choice being given to kids. Each year, the kids are getting fatter . . . Added to this, kids can now choose if they want to participate in sports – and many of them choose not to.'[3]

Developmental psychologists are starting to report something that wouldn't exactly be described as music to the ears of Toys R Us. They say that limiting the number of toys or games to a very small number is much better for our children, while more choice may actually damage their development. Having too many toys (too many choices) can make a child more timid and unsure, so that they play in short bursts with different toys and become unable to stick to, say, one or two for any length of time. And they don't enjoy their playing as much, spending less time playing in total than those children with fewer toys. It also means that their imagination is not brought into play either. The sheer number of choices overwhelms and overstimulates children, so they find it hard to concentrate on one thing long enough to learn from it. Instead, they simply shut down.

As a point of comparison, spending time with grandparents as opposed to consumer goods or media will work to our children's benefit. It's often grandparents who actually remember how to fire a child's imagination using books, telling stories or having conversations with a grandchild as opposed to that child relying on external variety and choice in the form of electronic media or consumer goods for stimulation. Grandparents also have the time and patience that modern, time-poor, overworked parents do not.

And by spending time with grandparents, children continue to be parented, albeit in a different way, and will learn to relate to and consider others because they have spent time relating to others – their grandparents – as opposed to things.

Money and tacit permission have ostensibly empowered our children, giving them choices and a latitude unknown by previous generations, so that they now have choices and a say in many things they previously wouldn't have had. Yet this transition has actually disempowered them. Democratic parenting coupled with child consumerism has given our children a sense of entitlement, and when people don't get from you what they assume they are entitled to, they tend to make life more difficult for you, and perhaps for others as well.

The gift of boredom

Our culture suffers from a phobia of a child being – God forbid – 'understimulated'. Allowing our children to entertain and pacify themselves with few, if any, external props is often misconstrued as being, in some way, neglectful. And yet giving our children the gift of boredom is one of the greatest contributions we can ever make as parents – not quite as high-ranking as unconditional love and affection, but a requirement if ever there was one. We need to reverse the assumption that options are good for childhood and entertain the distinct likelihood that choice today is actually retarding. Children will benefit tremendously from being allowed to learn how to stimulate themselves, using their own imagination and resourcefulness. This fosters a form of emotional and intellectual self-sufficiency, a skill that will provide them with enormous advantages in every area from school to marital relationships. Our children are being deprived of the right to be bored, and, in turn, deprived of learning the process to escape that boredom. It's the cognitive equivalent of preventing any physical exertion in our children to the point that they become unfit through never having had to exert themselves. If boredom produces self-sufficiency in our children, that self-sufficiency naturally militates against entitlement and any demanding expectations of you as a parent, and of others in general. In other words, it prevents children from being spoilt and acting in spoilt ways.

The statute of limitations

One important aspect of offering more choice and latitude to our child is that we are handing our child a perceived sense of greater control. Yet, ironically, this can serve to make our child feel less parented and less cared for, while at the same time making yet one more rod for our own backs – a child with a sense of entitlement to alternatives and negotiations over those alternatives.

Because a child consciously prefers to have a choice in everything, it doesn't, by any stretch of the imagination, mean that subconsciously they don't crave and need the opposite. This is, yet again, one more example of why parents are called parents, children are called children and why parents are trusted to make decisions in their children's best interests, not in response to their children's superficial demands. The Achilles heel to this principle is to be found in the many modern, overworked parents who are exhausted and often carry a subconscious sense of guilt. Allowing their children to entertain notions of choice is, for parents, a way of bestowing tolerance when they feel their children have been in some way deprived. Of course, thinking about it rationally, there isn't a quid pro quo resolution to a lack of 'quality time' with a child. Compensation isn't possible in this form. The greatest recompense would be for parents to override their exhaustion and guilt and 'disappoint' their children by limiting their choices anyway.

Today's compensation culture extends far beyond the industrial tribunal and payment is made in currencies ranging from pocket money and consultation over things there shouldn't be, to 'benefits' from piano, karate, riding and dance lessons. Children today are left with very few 'undesignated' moments in their lives.

And compensation culture isn't restricted to yuppies; divorce and separation have been a marvellous breeding ground for cultivating our children's sense of entitlement and their talent for claiming their benefits.

Spheres of influence

The areas in which children have choices and influences where they shouldn't are so numerous and wide-ranging, an entire book would be needed just to list them all. But perhaps the best way to get a handle on the tyranny of options in your children's lives is to stop and reflect: close your eyes and take a deep breath. In fact, take many, many deep breaths because you're going to need them when you realise just how much the tail has been wagging the dog. And, by the way, we are not the tail here. (You may want to write the list down on a piece of paper, look at it once, then burn it quickly.) There are a couple of everyday examples that can serve as parenting parables.

As I mentioned above, choice can lead to obesity. Yet again, the dinner table is more than a simple, flat surface: it is a veritable arena for socialisation to take place; a family micro-climate where lessons are learnt in areas that go far beyond what's on our children's plates. By now, few of us remain unaware that Britain's children are almost the fattest on earth, with rising levels of Type 2 diabetes in age groups that simply should not be experiencing this. But one aspect of this that is under-recognised is the level of autonomy that children have in deciding what enters their mouths: cake, biscuits, sweets, crisps, sugary drinks, ice cream, chips . . . You get the picture. They get the calories.

This has to do with a combination of rising levels of pocket money over the past decade, coupled with the increased avail-ability of cheap junk food, and topped with a lack of parental supervision. But even when it is the parents who buy and pre-pare the food, and the setting is the family meal, be it breakfast, lunch or dinner, there is an added dynamic: parental acquies-cence in the face of our children's imperious posture towards what's offered to them on a plate. As far as I can remember, chil-dren could always be 'fussy eaters' and mothers, in particular, have always had to contend with the issue of getting the broccoli down little Johnny's throat. The difference nowadays, however, is that little Johnny has tasted myriad options on his own before he even gets to the table. He has gastronomic points of compar-ison – many of them coming with lashings of MSG – that previous generations can only dream of. By the time he sits down to confront the dreary offerings he is presented with at home, he has had his taste buds primed and these offerings often pale by comparison. Even the most assertive and capable domes-tic goddesses often fret at the sight of their children not eating their breakfast before they go to school, or their lovingly pre-pared dinner when they come home. And when Johnny turns his nose up, or refuses to open his mouth (for a change), his mother feels beholden, often trying various ploys and even recipes to entice him to open his mouth in the right way at the right time (for a change). This is a recipe for disaster, not just there and then, at that particular meal, but in the wider scheme of things. Johnny is learning many unintended lessons, such as who is boss, what he is entitled to, that every aspect of his life is accom-panied by choices and, most unfortunate for his mother, why his refusal to eat tugs directly at her heartstrings. If Johnny were a girl, he would acquire an even greater understanding of how food and its rejection affords her tremendous power – the eating disorders' best friend.

But just in terms of the so-called obesity epidemic, countless parents will supply their children with food that they know is bad in the belief that any food is better than no food. And this way of thinking is reflected in the child's lunchbox too: better to give Johnny things he'll like and eat, than a healthy sandwich he'll leave untouched; after all, there's so much peer pressure – so crisps and a chocolate bar and a squash-type drink are bound to go down better than a healthy lunch. I was heartened to hear, at a recent meeting of health professionals involved in child nutrition, from two teachers of younger children in inner-city schools who described how they confiscate the lunchbox contraband provided by so many parents. And they actually see this as a form of child protection, against a culture that leads parents to inadvertently damage their children's health for life. One of them said, 'They simply shouldn't be allowed to have these choices.' How authoritarian, I thought; how wonderful.

If you're wondering how a remote middle-class professional like me can possibly understand these food issues, I should explain that I have to contend with this like anyone else, seven nights a week. My wife's a terrible cook. In fact, she hates her own cooking more than I do. On one occasion, she slammed her knife and fork down, and said of her own creation: 'This is so awful I can't eat any more!'

Fortunately, I enjoy cooking, and although one or two of my children do sometimes try it on when I cook dinner, it's quite clear to me that animals don't starve themselves. So while I may get irritated, I don't worry if they don't eat. But one thing I have learnt is that limiting their choices greatly improves my life and their diets. It has also been immensely helpful in influencing their general behaviour for the better and preventing a sense of entitlement. So, as an example, try waiting until they're very hungry for dinner, then serve them only the broccoli first. If they have several things on their plate and one of them happens to be chips, it is obvious that broccoli will be last in the queue, but this way you limit their points of comparison.

Depriving our children of points of comparison – be it on

their plate or in other areas – is the most positive form of deprivation we can bestow upon them. Obviously, there are certain foods that one or two of my children really hate, and I try to remain sensitive to these, but the general principle remains, and it works.

We have to act as gatekeepers, and, in the same way that we must censor what they see on television or on the Internet, we need to exercise nutritional censoring. Things that were considered treats in a previous generation have now become integral food choices, and children now feel *entitled* to incorporate these into their daily intake. If we restore the appropriate status to these foods – that of recreational food: a treat – our children will learn to consider them as such. And this gastronomic example is a parable in establishing control and authority, while eschewing entitlement, in other areas of our children's lives.

The nature of the beast

Away from the refrigerator, our children's sphere of influence and choices have led to further changes in their lives and their behaviour. In Aldous Huxley's *Brave New World,* 'It was decided to abolish the love of nature, at any rate among the lower classes ... We condition the masses to hate the country ... hence those electric shocks.'[4] New research gives credence to Huxley's dire prophecy. However, the electric shocks weren't needed.

Across the industrialised world, there has been a decline in children's contact with nature. A sixteen-year study in the US recently found a 25 per cent drop in visits to the countryside in the past twenty years, and a similar picture emerged from academics' research in Spain and Japan.[5] A further study in 2007 of 1000 pupils across England, commissioned by the Year of Food and Farming, found that one in five never visits the countryside and a further 17 per cent have only visited it once or twice.

Biologists Oliver Pergams and Patricia Zaradic, authors of the American study, pointed to 'a fundamental shift away from an appreciation of nature – biophilia – to videophilia, the new human tendency to focus on sedentary activities involving electronic media'.

Given the *choice*, most children will go for videophilia over biophilia because it provides more instant gratification, and that's what being a child is all about – if they can get away with it. However, it may surprise some people to hear that this isn't simply an environmental issue, and that a lack of contact with nature has altered our children's behaviours, contributing significantly to a spoilt generation.

One of the main barriers to establishing and exerting the necessary authority when dealing with children and young people nowadays is not a lack of compliance, but the difficulty in simply to get them to pay *attention* to what you have to say to start with. Their sensory systems have been indulged to the point that parents and teachers warrant little attention: they're a boring choice to attend to. Yet, if children don't bother to look at or listen to you, how can you parent, grandparent or teach effectively?

Well, the good news is that a growing number of scientists now believe that, for most of us, being exposed to greenery has general benefits for our ability to pay attention. Studies report 'superior attentional functioning' and that 'the effect of nature on inattention is robust'. A study published in the *American Journal of Public Health* found that exposing children with attention deficit hyperactivity disorder (ADHD) to outdoor greenery significantly reduced their symptoms. The scientists evaluated the effects of forty-nine after-school or weekend activities conducted in green outdoor settings, versus those conducted in built outdoor and indoor settings. The results were impressive and the effect was consistent across age, gender, socioeconomic status, type of community, geographic region and ADHD diagnosis: the greener the setting, the greater the relief from symptoms.[6]

In a new study by the same team (Frances Kuo and Andrea Faber Taylor of the University of Illinois), children aged between seven and twelve, all with ADHD were taken on twenty-minute walks in one of three environments – a city park and two other well-kept urban settings. The results were extraordinary: 'Effect sizes were substantial and comparable to those reported for recent formulations of methylphenidate (Ritalin). Conclusion: twenty minutes in a park setting was sufficient to elevate attention performance relative to the same amount of time in other settings.'[7]

What is highly important for all of us to realise is that these researchers also point to research conducted among people *without* ADHD, showing that inattention and impulsive behaviour are reduced after exposure to green, natural views and settings. Kuo and Taylor believe that 'views of green help girls foster life success'. In a study published in 2001, they randomly assigned 169 inner-city girls and boys to twelve architecturally identical high-rise buildings with varying levels of greenery in view near by. (As boys spent less time at home and played elsewhere, the results did not apply to them.) The researchers found that the greener and more natural a girl's view from home, the better she scored on tests of concentration, impulse inhibition and delayed gratification. They see this as happening through an improvement in 'self-discipline – a predictor of delinquency, drug abuse, poor school grades, teenage pregnancy'. Self-discipline requires your attention. So when your attentional system becomes tired, your self-discipline declines.[8] But how can something as mundane as a tree or some grass exert a biological effect? While the information-processing demands, multi-tasking and electronic distractions of everyday life cause attentional fatigue, it seems that greenery provides 'attentional restoration'. An ongoing study by the Netherlands Institute for Health Services Research on the important role of greenery in the daily lives of the population, entitled 'Vitamin G: effects of green space on health, wellbeing, and social safety', reports that 'research has shown that views of nature can improve feelings of neighbourhood safety and even lead to decreases in aggression and crime rates . . . and improved social cohesion'.[9]

Dr Tina Waliczek Cade from the Department of Agriculture at Texas State University conducted a study of 120,000 children and found that gardening increases their self-esteem and reduces the degree of stress they experience.[10] While videophilia feeds disregard, entitlement, instant gratification and impatience, children learn caring, responsibility and the ability to defer gratification by thinking in the longer term through watching the development of something they have planted.

So, exposure to nature provides significant physical, behavioural and intellectual benefits for children that reach deep into the home and the classroom, making it easier for parents and teachers to parent and teach.

In addition, while the recreation of choice for children of today stimulates their stress-producing sympathetic nervous system, greenery activates the opposite parasympathetic nervous system, which calms and relaxes them; it helps to socialise them if you like. Greenery can wean them off their growing need for the constant high stimulation of mass variety, choice and sources of the buzz. It's even used to help treat drug addiction.

Precisely how exposing our children to the green life socialises them into becoming better-behaved human beings is still not clear. However, as Edward O. Wilson, the Harvard University biologist, explained when he introduced his theory of biophilia in the early 1980s, humans are hard-wired to gravitate towards greenery. Our ancestors, who sought green areas or lived as subsistence hunters, gatherers and farmers, were more likely to eat, drink and survive. Today, many of the benefits associated with our exposure to greenery may be part of an evolutionary reward system reinforcing the very thing that kept us alive for hundreds of thousands of years. Future choice in our children's lives should revolve more around the colour green: more outdoor play time, greener playgrounds, more plants at home and in schools, school and family gardening, trips to the countryside or just a walk in the park. Some scientists refer to a recommended daily allowance for our children of twenty minutes spent among greenery, which may seem bizarre as a parenting 'technique', but which does have increasing scientific justification.

Seeing green should become less of a choice and more of a straightforward requirement – like food and sleep.

No option

More generally, children should not only have fewer choices, but should not feel entitled to have *any* choices whatsoever in some areas of their lives. To create a braver new world, parents, child-minders, teachers and grandparents should all consider the various domains of a child's life and think consciously about where they feel that child has too much choice. In many cases – whether concerning food, activities, toys, clothing – we can limit our children's choices and their sense of entitlement to them by simply not allowing certain choices to enter the house, the room, the discussion or our children's heads to begin with. In others, it involves convincing ourselves that we have a right to limit or remove choices, to take a deep breath, just say 'No', and mean it.

Ten

Bigging Them Up
Misinterpreting self-esteem

Oscar Levant – pianist, film star and wit – stood by at a party, as George Gershwin spent the entire evening at the piano playing his own music and clearly having a great time. Finally, he could contain himself no longer, and enquired, indelicately: 'Tell me, George, if you had to do it all over again, would you still fall in love with yourself?'

If the nineteenth century was the age of hysteria, we, in this day and age, are living an ongoing love affair with self-esteem. The origins of the term self-esteem are a bit unclear; some believe John Milton first coined this term over 350 years ago, and while we would be more likely to believe it first reached prominence on the pages of the *San Francisco Self-Express* in the 1960s, its public debut is said to have taken place in a very, very different climate: the *Manchester Examiner* in 1884.

At first, self-esteem related to children as individuals but more recently the concept has been extended to include notions of collective self-esteem – how particular 'minority' groups feel about themselves. In fact, in order to improve the behaviour of young people, social engineering was directed at increasing their self-esteem by the California Task Force to Promote Self-Esteem and Personal and Social Responsibility. The politicians, along with many experts, predicted that increasing self-esteem could help to solve a wide variety of personal and social problems and behaviour, from crime and children failing at school to domestic violence. In fact, its main supporter, Assemblyman John Vasconcellos, in a divine leap of faith, hoped that higher self-esteem would ultimately balance the state budget, based upon the observation that those with high self-regard have higher incomes and therefore pay more tax.

But, as Professor Roy F. Baumeister, the prolific researcher on self-esteem, laments surprisingly: 'A generation – and many millions of dollars – later, it turns out we may have been mistaken . . . the American Psychological Society commissioned me and several other experts to wade with an open mind through the enormous amount of published research on the subject and to assess the benefits of high self-esteem. Here are some of our disappointing findings.' And, even I, who have watched with unease as a spoilt generation has emerged, high on unconditional praise and reward, was surprised at the emphatic nature of these findings.

Firstly, 'High self-esteem in schoolchildren does not produce better grades.' It seems, if anything, it's the other way around: getting good grades leads to higher self-esteem. In fact, a study at Virginia Commonwealth University found that university students with mediocre grades, who received frequent self-esteem strokes from their lecturers, ended up doing worse in their final exams than students who were told to bite the bullet and try harder.

In adults, higher self-esteem doesn't lead them to perform better at their jobs either. Although people with high self-esteem rate their own job performance better – even describing themselves as brighter and more attractive than their peers with low self-esteem – neither objective tests nor impartial judges can find any difference in the quality of work. And outside the work-place, those with high self-esteem think they make better impressions, have stronger friendships and have better romantic lives than other people, 'but the data don't support their self-flattering views. If anything, people who love themselves too much sometimes annoy other people by their defensive or know-it-all attitudes.' Baumeister also points to the findings that self-esteem doesn't predict who will make a good leader, and that some work has found humility rather than self-esteem to be a crucial trait in successful leaders.

It has often been assumed that it is low self-esteem that is more likely to be a cause of violence, 'but in reality, violent individuals, groups and nations think very well of themselves'. People with high self-esteem are likely to respond aggressively when their inflated view of themselves is threatened by criticism or perceived insult, or when someone obstructs their need for gratification. You can see why any discussion of spoilt children has to rethink our preconceptions about self-esteem.

Members of gangs are found to have high self-esteem, so do wife-beaters. Violent criminals, who we've been told are 'acting out' their low self-esteem, actually have the highest scores on a personality scale of narcissism (excessive self-love). And high self-esteem has been linked to bullying, 'according to most of the studies that have been done; it is simply untrue that beneath the surface of every obnoxious bully is an unhappy, self-hating child in need of sympathy and praise'. High self-esteem doesn't prevent children and young people from cheating, stealing or experimenting with drugs and sex. Children with high self-esteem may be even more willing to try these things at a young age.

Baumeister's conclusion is unequivocal:

In short, despite the enthusiastic embrace of self-esteem, we found that it conferred only two benefits. It feels good and it supports initiative. Those are nice, but they are far less than we had once hoped for, and it is very questionable whether they justify the effort and expense that schools, parents and therapists have put into raising self-esteem. After all these years, I'm sorry to say, my recommendation is this: Forget about self-esteem and concentrate more on self-control and self-discipline. Recent work suggests this would be good for the individual and good for society – and might even be able to fill some of those promises that self-esteem once made but could not keep.[1]

While I continue to use the expression 'self-esteem' as convenient shorthand for 'self-confidence', I too have great reservations about our wholehearted embrace of bigging our children up in the undiscerning way we have.

Furthermore, as with our understanding of cholesterol levels, research on high self-esteem is now finding that there are good and bad forms. For example, a recent study in the *Journal of Personality* broke high self-esteem down into 'secure versus fragile' types, whereby fragile self-esteem was defined as more unstable or variable. The study concluded that high self-esteem isn't necessarily healthy self-esteem. 'There are many kinds of high self-esteem, and in this study we found that for those in which it is fragile and shallow, it's no better than having low self-esteem,' says researcher Michael Kernis, Professor of Psychology at the University of Georgia. 'People with fragile high self-esteem compensate for their self-doubts by engaging in exaggerated tendencies to defend, protect and enhance their feelings of self-worth.'[2] It's now becoming clear that of the multiple forms of high self-esteem, only some consistently relate to positive psychological functioning. This research is revealing what none of us wanted to hear: that high self-esteem per se can make people very unlikeable when others (or events) threaten their egos.

Ego inflation

It seems that when our culture fell in love with the idea of raising self-esteem, we forgot to consider exactly what kind of self we were trying to raise the esteem of. This has been a significant oversight, akin to starting construction to erect a new building without first taking into account what the raw materials, the foundations, are made of. The received wisdom has put the cart before the horse, promoting greater self-esteem in some children whose sense of self is distorted and damaged, thereby creating a narcissistic entitled child. The religion of enhancing self-esteem is devoted to expressing feelings and emotions, without, at the same time, demanding self-discipline and self-control – civilised behaviour.

A selfish vocabulary of the self has been born of this trend. Terms that imply responsibility or accountability for the self, such as self-criticism, self-discipline, self-control, self-effacement, self-reproach and self-sacrifice, are being nudged aside by more positive terms of endearment for the self – self-expression, self-assertion, self-indulgence, self-realisation, self-acceptance, self-love and, of course, self-esteem.

Constructive criticism has acquired a bad image. Many parents have shied away from shaping their children's development, avoiding criticism for fear that it will undermine their child's self-esteem. Armed with a blanket belief that what children need is approval, they have gone on an approval spree, sanctioning – or at least overlooking – many aspects of their children's behaviour that should be met with disapproval. This is partly driven by a misunderstanding of what a child's identity is and an erroneous belief that disapproval stunts the development of a child's sense of self; that it hinders what would naturally flourish. But, yet again, a reluctance to disapprove has also come about as a by-product of the absent parent: long working hours, divorce and separation provide the breeding ground for inaction and approval where, often, the opposite is needed in order to do right by a child.

At the school gates in the morning, I often see something that could have come straight out of a sickly American feelgood movie: burly fathers kissing their sons and gushing, 'Love youuuu!' I mention this because I often sense an element of compensation in the parent's voice, or faint evidence that he is trying to do the right thing. And, of course, there's no reason why telling your child publicly that you love them should not be the right thing; but this often fits in with a bigger picture of Britain's tentative footsteps towards emotional literacy, of parents making grand gestures of approval and affection, while retreating from disapproving of or standing up to their children's unacceptable behaviour.

None the less, like boundaries and consequences, disapproval is required (albeit not feelgood) parenting and should not be problematic if our children's sense of self is nourished at a far more fundamental level.

The public debut of the self

Defining the 'self' is an ongoing problem that has kept philosophers and scientists busy for centuries. The self is certainly abstract. However, it's a useful tool with which to reflect on the failings of the self-esteem movement, so I only use it in this sense.

The greatest paradox in the age of the self is that the more we promote it, the weaker it often becomes. A primary development in our culture has been greater self-expression and self-exposure as a means to supposedly connect to others, thereby receiving a greater appreciation and acknowledgement of the self. The more extreme examples involve the so-called misery memoirs, through which unknowns and well-knowns alike share the most private compartments of the self with people they don't know. This same fashion occurs, increasingly, in all areas of the media. One publisher recently asked me, rhetorically: 'Where's it going to end? I mean, being only sexually abused isn't enough nowadays; it has to come with bells and whistles.'

And celebrities who, at one time, would hire teams of image bodyguards to keep private information from the public gaze, now queue up to sob on television, radio and in print about their abortions, sexual problems, ongoing drug dependency, cosmetic surgery, gastric bands, and so on. One well-known BBC television presenter whose career was stalling appeared naked in the foetal position, being flushed on a colonic irrigation table, for, supposedly, an informative documentary. Revealing one's inner secrets continues to take on more and more graphic forms. The late Jade Goody's intimate sharing of the final weeks, days and hours leading up to her death from cancer broke further boundaries of privacy and discretion.

There is an erroneous belief that it is good to give of yourself, in every sense, publicly, in order to receive; that if you allow strangers inside your psyche and other parts of your self, larger and larger numbers of people will like you, while at the same time, the process is therapeutic for you. It's a win–win situation.

This mindset transcends social class. Diana, Princess of Wales, Prince Charles and Bill Clinton shared the same public therapist's couch as the lowest of the déclassé and seemed to feel perfectly comfortable. As a health professional trying to write books that offer helpful information, it's been made clear to me by publishers that most of the money available to non-fiction writers is earmarked for the abused or the celebrity flashers. I thought about striking a deal with my father whereby I claim he did unspeakable things to me, I get a lucrative book deal with a ghostwriter thrown in and my dad and I split the proceeds . . .

I YouTube, therefore I AM

At a more pedestrian level, a new generation competes to construct their online identities and share many of their intimate 'secrets' with those of others. Despite the ubiquitous term 'self', there has actually been a great cultural pressure to avoid, even erode, what would constitute a real self and, instead, to objectify ourselves as entities we can and should stand apart from and examine before polishing and returning to the mantelpiece.

After careful deliberation, children now construct their public identity for social networking sites and upload videos of themselves to YouTube. As they begin so-called 'social networking' at younger and younger ages and for more hours per day, their perspective on what constitutes the self is being distorted, precisely because of this emphasis on objectifying themselves. Their true ability to 'get in touch with their emotions' is being interfered with because they're always looking over their shoulder to the sea of gazes from their 'friends' on Facebook, Twitter, Bebo, etc.

At the same time, they're lacking the required gazes from their own parents and siblings, ideally in the mutual form of interplay. This is thought to help children to value themselves highly, but accurately, because they have a reliable 'feedback' system and unconditional love on tap from judges they can trust.

However, problems begin to develop when children are ignored – perhaps as a result of their parents' continual preoccupation with other things. This may sound like yet another philosophical diatribe, but it has direct implications on how our children develop and how they feel about themselves and others. If we truly want to boost our children's self-esteem by reinforcing and nourishing their sense of self, we have to protect them from invading their own privacy and giving their self away.

Privacy is fundamental to what constitutes who we are, our identity, the 'self'. Yet in our society our children have less and less sense of it. By sharing their private self in the way they are increasingly doing, they erode the individual. In a culture that is showing such concern for privacy in other areas, such as data protection, this is ironic. Privacy is a fundamental part of democracy. As the

Czech writer Milan Kundera once wrote about being spied on in a police state: 'Private and public are two essentially different worlds and respect for that difference is the indispensable condition for a man to live free . . .'

For parents, at a practical level, allowing our children to spend as much time as possible in the real, as opposed to the virtual, world of the self will allow them to develop a more authentic self. For a child to build up a strong sense of identity, we have to reduce the level of distraction that is enticing them to focus on the external at the expense of the internal. Yet our market-led culture demands the opposite: consumers looking *outward* to saleable temptations, because there's certainly no profit to be made from encouraging self-reflection or developing a child's inner landscape. In this, it is less a case of actively parenting and more a case of clearing the way for our children to develop more naturally and more healthily. We are quick to condemn 'stage mothers' who push their children to create and present a polished public persona, which is then presented for judgement during their vulnerable and fragile developmental years. Yet there is now a similar threat to a greater number of our children online, this time not because parents are overly involved in pushing their children's public image, but because they are *not* actively involved while their children are busy creating and presenting their own polished public persona.

To be fair, this technology and the preoccupation with it are so new that we weren't to know the implications for abstract concepts such as the self, but when it comes to our children's welfare, the best rule of thumb should always be 'first do no harm', or, better safe than sorry. This technology is obviously the future, and part of a much bigger media and celebrity culture in which our children feel they have to perform with one eye on a virtual audience they may not even know. But that doesn't mean we shouldn't try to minimise its impact on them. There is always the inevitable outcry over this in the sensational cases of girls being groomed and taken abroad by Internet paedophiles, of teenage suicides supported by virtual communities or school massacres in which the teenage killer(s) create a virtual profile to accompany their story. But the real risk to our children is far more mundane and insidious; it is the risk that our children are not leading their lives but are presenting their lives in private.

Ministry of the self

The ongoing efforts to enhance the self-esteem of sections of society deemed to be deprived or disadvantaged should be re-examined. The current obsession with 'people of diversity' (PODs) is instructive in collective spoiling. In both the United States and in Britain, there is growing unease about the effect of positive discrimination on the PODs it's intended to enhance the self-esteem of.

One problem is that advantage is being bestowed by the empowered anointed upon the disadvantaged benighted – a dynamic which, itself, carries with it the baggage of a servant–master relationship along with charity and victimhood. The other problem is our cowardly avoidance of sanctioning and condemning the unacceptable behaviour of those we pity or feel guilty about because of their deprivation both material and in terms of self-esteem in our view. Like a spoilt child whose parents' overriding concern is not to impede their self-esteem, we continue to tolerate levels of behaviour and crime, including murder, partly in the name of enhancing collective self-esteem. In Britain, crime figures and the 'diversity' of the perpetrator are hard to come by (and are often described as 'highly sensitive . . . we have to be very careful . . . we can't draw any conclusions from these figures . . . '). Like the individual child, tolerating bad behaviour and high crime levels in the belief that you have to make allowances because of past injustices and the need to enhance a public sense of self is an abdication of responsibility of the worst kind. Truly to enhance the identity and sense of self of disadvantaged sections of society, we must allow them to be treated like members of society and therefore subject them to the same expectations and requirements in their civil behaviour as all other citizens: that is, treat them equally. High expectations are better for the self.

Cut the self down to size

It is no coincidence that in the 'repressive years', when parents and teachers used to naturally reinforce humility and modesty, as opposed to unjustified pride, our children were far better behaved and respected authority. Children who are repeatedly told that there is nothing about themselves that demands improvement – or as some American schools advertise on large banners in their hallways: 'I am one of the most special people in the whole wide world' – are being helped to develop a distorted, socially unviable sense of self. On the other hand, parents and teachers who set realistically high expectations, criticise when it is warranted and are intolerant of egotistical behaviour and values are doing children and the rest of us a great favour, boosting our authority and children's wellbeing.

Whether parent, child or the most unfortunate of minority groups, the next time we hear self-esteem-boosting catch phrases such as, 'because I'm worth it', 'be good to yourself' or 'I deserve to win', we could all do with pausing for thought.

Eleven

The Devil's Buttermilk

The special role of alcohol in child development

Adolescent and teenage parenting guides today tend to treat underage drinking as a consequence or a symptom of an underlying problem, rather than something that can actually change the way in which a child develops respect for authority and for others. And few people seem to recognise that there is actually a neurochemical dimension to the issues of spoilt children and lack of respect for authority.

The human brain is still in the process of development until around the age of twenty-four, and is more susceptible to damage than the adult brain. In adolescents who regularly drink alcohol, parts of the brain important in emotional and impulse control have actually been found to be smaller. It's important to hear the dry, clinical language of the scientific findings to bring some sobriety to the comfy view of teenagers 'enjoying a drink'. For example 'alcohol use during adolescence is associated with prefrontal volume abnormalities, including white matter differences',[1] or, the 'neurotoxic effects of alcohol on adolescent . . . corpus callosum microstructural injury'.[2] These findings provide a glimpse of the neurological landscape of alcohol's role in preventing teenagers from developing self-control when they're sober, because their brain hardware is underdeveloped.

Whether in moderation or excess, adults drink alcohol because it disinhibits those parts of the brain that have evolved over many years to control our thoughts, feelings and behaviours. Of course, most adults prefer to view this less technically in terms of 'relaxing' and 'enjoying ourselves'. And, in most cases, this is what it does. Yet alcohol's extraordinary ability to disinhibit our other adult impulses is well documented every day of the week. In Britain, alcohol is associated with 60–70 per cent of homicides, 70 per cent of stabbings, 70 per cent of beatings and 50 per cent of fights or assaults in the home. Violent offenders are much more likely to be heavy drinkers than demographically matched samples of the general population.[3] And beyond the murders and stabbings, rapes and wife beatings, there's the more off-the-shelf forms of boorish, entitled behaviour – from extreme rudeness to cat fights and pub brawls – exhibited by adults, available all hours, compliments of alcohol, the grand disinhibitor.

We need only look at the role of alcohol in the spoilt and antisocial behaviour of adults to realise that there's no reason why it should not help our children to become badly behaved too. But the effects on the young are, in fact, far more fundamental: when children and teenagers drink, the disinhibition that takes place does so at a point when their brains and behaviours are still undergoing crucial development of the ability to *control* impulses, so disrupting this essential process.

When children drink, they are not only being allowed to do something which you both know is primarily an adult 'privilege', they are also relinquishing control of their thoughts, feelings and behaviour with your blessing. By the time they are sixteen, many, if not most, teenagers feel entitled to drink and to get (technically) drunk. And they are learning that an abdication of responsibility is acceptable when they are relaxed or 'tipsy', provided 'it's the drink talking'. Allowing children to be under the influence with our consent offers them mixed messages regarding self-control and personal accountability at a time when they need a clear, unambiguous one. And driving a teenager to a pub, or buying alcoholic drinks for their unchaperoned party, supports them in disregarding rules and the law, with the albeit unintended effect of undermining authority, including our own.

Pub people

Having visited a wide variety of unusual places, it's clear to me that drinking occupies a special cultural place in Britain and northern Europe. In many communities, the pub is treated as the neighbourhood sitting room, a place where children are welcome. Even underage teens can go into a pub by themselves, sit and drink soft drinks.

In addition to this, there is a general belief that the early introduction of 'responsible' drinking at home (see p. 162) will, in some way, prevent heavy drinking later. And because drinking is such an integral part of adult life, we feel uneasy when this comfortable, 'sensible' view of drinking is turned upside down and challenged. However, a new crop of studies is doing exactly this – you may need a stiff drink before reading on!

Effects of alcohol

International comparative studies are finding that British children are more likely to get drunk than those of any other country.[4, 5] A new study of fifteen- and sixteen-year-olds in thirty-five countries reports that British children are among the worst binge drinkers in Europe, with direct effects on their relationships with their parents. The European School Survey Project on Alcohol and Other Drugs reported that 'serious problems with parents, serious problems with friends and physical fights . . . were related to their alcohol consumption'. One of the authors said: 'The UK retains its unenviable position in relation to binge drinking, intoxication and alcohol-related problems amongst teenagers. This problem is both serious and chronic. I hope that the government will prioritise policies that are effective to reduce heavy drinking and alcohol-related disorders and health problems amongst young people.'[6]

And child alcoholics are a growing problem, with an increasing number being treated in hospital every day for alcohol-related illnesses, including mental disorders, alcohol poisoning and liver disease. Professor Ian Gilmore, President of the Royal College of Physicians, has described this trend as: 'a staggering rise and it is only the tip of the iceberg . . . the younger they drink, the more likely they are to have alcohol-related problems later in life. It is now commonplace to see men and women in their twenties with end-stage alcoholic liver damage.'[7] While there is a host of problems waiting for young heavy drinkers when they're older, other problems need less time to develop.

The Alcohol Research Consortium has a different way of measuring alcohol's influence on young people's attitudes to authority and to one another: 'Our ultimate aim is to try and reduce the incidence of facial trauma sustained as a result of alcohol and violence.' Just looking at the gruesome gaping and bleeding faces published in their papers and in medical journals such as the *British Journal of Oral Maxillofacial Surgery*[8] gives one an immediate graphic sense of what the headlines and statistics have been saying for a long time. The job of these surgeons is to put torn faces back together again when possible. Their cutting-edge industry has to contend with 'the complex link between alcohol and violence'.[3]

Authoritarian line on drugs

Interestingly, Britain's attitude towards drugs has been reasonably priggish. Prime ministers and political wannabes are concerned about whether the media will discover or even ask, 'Did you inhale a quarter of a century ago when you were at Oxford?' Yet in contrast, most of them would be embarrassed to be accused by the media of having been stone-cold sober throughout their university years, and their spin doctors would be called in to create retrospective socially acceptable anecdotes of the jolly drunkenness experienced by the in-touch-with-today's-youth politician. Adults love alcohol and governments collect extraordinary levels of sin tax from it, while at the same time pointing to drugs as the greatest menace to our children and their behaviour. But alcohol always has been and continues to be, by far, our children's greatest drug problem.

A study in the *Lancet* ranking twenty of Britain's most popular drugs places alcohol at number five among the most dangerous substances – far higher than ecstasy, LSD, solvents, amphetamines and cannabis.[9] And while everyone still remembers the name Leah Betts, fourteen years after her death, as well as the ill-advised and dishonest campaigns telling children that 'ecstasy kills', few of us know the name of a single child or young person who has died of alcohol poisoning at *any* time in British or world history, even though there are tens of thousands of them. And there are no campaigns in any one of *their* names. Incidentally, it was subsequently discovered that the direct cause of Leah Betts's death was actually 'water intoxication', not drugs – but that's not what society wanted to hear or believe.

Date-rape drink

One of the contemporary indulgent behaviours decried by society is casual sex – even sex on the open pavement – among younger and younger girls, along with the highest levels of unwanted young pregnancies in Europe and all that goes with it. Parents and schools are desperate to regain some authority over children's sexual behaviour. While much debate surrounds how much sex education our children should have and at what age, few people understand the enormous role that alcohol plays in sexual behaviour. Which is extraordinary, considering that there are few male parents, teachers and politicians who haven't used alcohol strategically to get their leg over. And alcohol is consistently cited as greatly increasing the incidence of unwanted pregnancies and sexually transmitted diseases in adults, not to mention in our children. The latest misguided exaggeration is directed towards the witch-hunt for 'spiked' drinks and 'date-rape' drugs. Yet consultants and biochemists who conducted medical studies of blood and urine samples from young females attending hospital accident and emergency departments, claiming that their drinks had been 'spiked' with date-rape drugs, concluded: 'No one tested positive for rohypnol or GHB. The symptoms are more likely to be a result of excess alcohol.'[10] Another similar study found: 'A large number of study participants had serum ethanol concentrations associated with significant intoxication.'[11] So, it seems, we find it hard to accept the obvious: that drinks do not have to be spiked with 'date-rape' drugs for women to be drugged and date-raped – alcohol has always been a highly effective date-rape drug in its own right.

Obviously, the other part of this equation is that boys' libido, along with their impulse control, is also powerfully disinhibited when they're drunk before that impulse control is fully formed. They are more likely to 'date-rape', or be falsely accused of either that or sexual assault, if they have been drinking.

Little, early and often to avoid disappointment?

Despite the direct links between alcohol and big problems for our children and their behaviour and attitude towards authority, it is only recently that the penny has begun to drop. Even doctors and nurses that I know have been carried along with the assumption that the best way to prevent our children from drinking heavily – and behaving badly as a result – is to teach them to drink while they are children. This assumption has been heavily promoted by educational bodies that appear to be impartial but are, in fact, funded by the drinks industry, and are well versed in the comfy-speak of 'teaching children sensible drinking' or 'responsible drinking'.

In England, one prep school was reported to have asked a local wine merchant in to give forty twelve-year-old pupils a class, 'Wines of the World', in which the children were invited to taste various wines.[12] We don't recommend early, sensible dope smoking to prevent later drug abuse, early cigarette smoking to prevent later nicotine addiction or early sexual encounters to prevent unwanted pregnancy. But when it comes to our logic regarding introducing children to alcohol, we seem to be thinking under the influence of alcohol. Our complacency sees child and teenage drinking as inevitable, but it is only inevitable because we not only allow it to be, but, inadvertently, make it so.

A new study commissioned by the Department for Children, Schools and Families cites the myth regarding the benefits of the continental approach to introducing children gradually to alcohol as a 'huge obstacle' to overcome. 'The misperceptions are firmly based on opinion rather than from health statistics about mainland Europe. Parents . . . are searching for any logic that helps them maintain their own drinking whilst protecting their children.'[13] Many parents just can't say 'No', and – wrongly – feel that they can't say, 'Do as I say, not as I do.' While, in fact, one the most fundamental differences between a parent and child is that a parent *can* do things that a child cannot: parent and child are *not* equal. This is further evidence of both parents and children being unable to accept the fundamental difference between the status of parent and child.

Although parents may delude themselves into believing that they are giving their children a more responsible cosmopolitan and sophisticated approach to alcohol, it is worth noting that France's death rate from cirrhosis of the liver is actually twice that of the UK's. 'Liver cirrhosis is caused by long-term excessive drinking by individuals, regardless of their drinking patterns.'[14] The point being, that while 'binge drinking' may be one particularly anti-social British route to health damage, even the slow, stylish continental way will get you there. No wonder that the organisation Alcohol Concern has called for parents who give alcohol to children under fifteen to be prosecuted.[15]

A new paper in the *British Journal of Psychiatry* reports that 'urgent action is needed' to prevent 'an under-recognised, alcohol-related . . . dementia time bomb' that is facing young drinkers.[16]

Somehow, however, the myth still persists that introducing our children to alcohol earlier prevents heavy drinking and alcoholism later. While many believe that children benefit from the role-modelling and restraint displayed at the family dinner table, they have not considered the *biochemical* processes at work. Exposure to alcohol at an early age is *more* likely to increase the chances of a child becoming a heavy drinker. A new study from the US government's National Institute on Alcohol Abuse and Alcoholism examined the history of 22,000 adults, and revealed that having a first taste of alcohol before the age of fifteen sharply increased 'the risk of alcohol-use disorders that persist into adulthood'. It found: '. . . early alcohol consumption itself, as a misguided choice or decision, is driving the relationship between early drinking and risk for development of later alcohol problems'. The researchers believe it is important to delay the 'age of first drink' as long as possible.[17] A young brain, as we have seen, is very malleable and changes quickly in response to new influences; it's suspected that early exposure may 'prime' the brain to enjoy alcohol by creating a link between it and pleasurable reward.

Against popular feeling, Sir Liam Donaldson, the UK's Chief Medical Officer, recommends that parents do not allow their children to consume alcohol at all – which includes having a drink at home – until they have reached, at least, the age of fifteen. He believes alcohol can seriously affect brain development in young people: 'We're trying to get the message across that children aged under fifteen are still developing, their brains are developing, and drinking alcohol can do some quite serious damage.'[18] This advice comes in stark contrast to the current law: it may surprise some parents to know that, at the time of writing, in the UK the legal drinking age for a child is five.

I continue to discover apparently considerate and intelligent parents who actually supply 'only wine and lager, but of course not any spirits because that's too strong' for their sixteen-year-old children's parties. Many feel referred peer pressure from their children, who claim that all their fourteen- or fifteen-year-old friends' parents supply alcohol at their birthday parties, 'and if you don't let me give my friends drinks at my birthday party then they won't come!' In one case, the parents went out for the evening, so as not to get in the way of the fun, only to be called back at midnight because their daughter was lying drunk and unconscious in a pool of vomit. There have also been occasions when I've rung up parents regarding my fifteen-year-old daughter spending the night at their home, only to be told: 'They're not here right now – they've gone on a pub crawl ... I think they're starting at the Hump and Pump and finishing off at the Loob and Boob.' In all cases, I've had no support from parents in trying to prevent fifteen-year-old girls either from going on pub crawls or being left at home with booze supplied by parents. And I've been made to feel a priggish killjoy.

But there are more everyday subtle examples.

Our local infant school regularly puts on Friday night discos for four-year-olds at which they create a kiddie nightclub setting. Apparently, it is felt that children should be taught to enjoy the same things that people several times their age do. It isn't the fact that there's disco music or that children are having a party. It is the inculcation of our children with a grown-up alcohol-related culture, priming them for an arena that is alcohol-dependent years before they're actually allowed into that arena.

And the other night, a ten-year-old girl was wistfully lamenting the fact that her mother had changed jobs; she missed the 'old days', she said, when she and her mother would go to the pub on a Friday night with her mother's work colleagues 'and we would have drinks and chat'. (I assume she was eight or nine at the time.)

Ironically, these are often the parents who filter their children's water and eschew GM or non-organic foods. What a paradox.

Changing our culture

We need to take a cold, hard, detached look at the cultural background that has prevented us from protecting our children from alcohol and the way it affects their social development, behaviour and attitude to authority. And such a re-examination is not going to be easy. This is partly because the majority of us are too close to the subject matter – as are many of our children's heroes. I routinely hear famous BBC Radio 1 DJs joking about how hammered they were the night before, as they read out emails and texts and take phone calls from freshly hung-over youths. They want to come across as 'edgy', but in reality they are nationalised, funky civil servants whose edginess comes at the taxpayer's cost.

So uncool and anally retentive is it considered to be a non-drinker; it's akin to spending your Friday night in the library – or in church, God forbid. There has to be something wrong with you if you don't want to drink, or if you don't want to go somewhere where most people get drunk. And the interesting thing about this kind of conformity is that it's supported by the most eclectic orgy-sized group of bedfellows, from the radical student unionist in their university-subsidised bar, to Nobby the neo-Nazi and his shaven-headed mates, to Brighton's pink-pounders to the House of Commons (where our MPs have a choice of twelve bars, subsidised by us taxpayers and where, apparently, when Peter Mandelson resigned for the second time, 'the bar ran out of champagne'.[19] As an enlightened-puritan American, more accustomed to healthy political pastimes involving Bill Clinton, kneeling women and 'inappropriate relationships' without a single drink being involved (at least, not on the part of the President), my discovery that many MPs had to be dragged drunk from the House of Commons bars in order to vote on matters of national importance is stranger than a *Monty Python* sketch.

The problem with conducting a sober discussion about the issue of alcohol's role in our children's socialisation is that Britain's heart simply isn't in it, so great is the long-standing affection for and the ubiquity of the nation's silly sauce.

Fortunately, however, there is a slight change in the air. The British government's Health Secretary has now acknowledged that: 'Non-drinkers are often subjected to the same disdain that non-smokers were thirty or forty years ago, when people looked at you strangely if you refused a cigarette. They are the odd ones out . . . the question we must ask as a society is why, unlike smoking, it is the abstainers that draw people's attention, not those who regularly drink their weekly limit in a day.'[20]

One of the more telling signs that alcohol really is an enormous issue in child development is the observation that in America politicians are now willing to forgo the tremendous amount of sin tax they would get from alcohol sales by raising the legal drinking age from eighteen to twenty-one. That speaks volumes. When Ben Kinsella, the brother of the *EastEnders* actress, was stabbed to death in London in 2008, causing an outcry over 'knife crime', society didn't ask: why was a sixteen-year-old boy in a pub at two o'clock in the morning? It seemed to be a cultural norm; people couldn't see the wood for the trees.

Time, gentlemen, please

Parents and other adults in authority need to be aware that *their* favourite drug and social lubricant may have new-found consequences when children indulge in it.

Recent evidence makes it abundantly clear that parents should not allow their children to consume alcohol at all – including having a drink at home – until they have reached at least the age of fifteen. We should have a single legal drinking age, even if it is unenforceable. This will send a new message to parents and society about what is good for our children, and will make it easier to exert authority over those of them who increasingly feel entitled to drink.

As a point of comparison, even though the US has fifty different states, each with its own laws, the federal government felt compelled to pass the National Minimum Drinking Age Act to override each state's individual laws. People under the age of twenty-one cannot buy alcohol, full stop. In addition, many states do not allow those under twenty-one to enter an off-licence or a bar, full stop. And many states do not allow anyone under twenty-one to drink anywhere, including home – in other words, alcohol consumption is banned completely before the age of twenty-one. Britain's approach of allowing five-year-olds to drink alcohol at home, and underage teenagers to sit in pubs where older teenagers can easily buy them drinks leaves too much room for confusion and manoeuvre. Enforcement agencies in the UK have been extremely unsuccessful in preventing off-licences, shops and pubs from selling children alcohol. And children often – although they shouldn't – feel entitled to be irritated when asked for proof of age. The signs in shops saying,

'Please do not be offended if we ask for proof of age when you buy alcohol' should be changed to: 'You MUST prove you are over eighteen or we will not sell you alcohol. Furthermore, if you try to buy it anyway, we'll call the police and beg them to arrest, jail and prosecute you.'

Many physicians and researchers, including the government's own Chief Medical Officer, now strongly believe that the government must raise the price of alcohol as a disincentive for both children and adults to buy it.

I don't know of any parents who allow their children to consider being a *non*-drinker when they grow up. We bow to what we see as the inevitable. But while children are developing, absorbing our values and ideas and looking at various options, we should include the possibility of a child being a non-drinker – where alcohol may be seen as fun but not as necessary to have fun – as one of those options.

From now on, we – parents, teachers and policy-makers alike – must be especially aware of where our information about alcohol education comes from; sadly most of it is the product of vested interests. We should raise our glasses to child sobriety, one of the main benefits of which will be to remove yet one more obstacle from our ability to parent with authority. And so it's high time we exorcised the Devil's buttermilk from our children's development.

Twelve

Dethroning the Emperors
Summary

Next time we see a version of that bumper sticker 'put children first', we should stop and think about what this throwaway line actually means and how it should be interpreted. Putting children first should mean putting adults – particularly parents – in charge. It should mean restoring authority, taking control and responsibility, and returning our little emperors to the civilian life they're genuinely entitled to. And there's plenty of rebuilding to be done.

An enlightened intolerance

It's not only authority that requires and is worthy of redemption – so too does that unpopular word 'intolerance'. We need a licence to feel confident about passing value judgements and not tolerating unacceptable behaviour – not only in our own children, but in other people's too.

There is an overriding necessity to reinstate boundaries and to work against our children developing an inflated sense of entitlement. Powered by love, these are basic tools with which we may shape our children's behaviour and attitudes. And so it's important to reflect on our own status as parents, teachers and that of anyone else who should be figures of authority, but who may have been seduced into offering children the hand of friendship in place of the firm hand of authority.

Spoiling starts at home with parenting, and while the term 'parents' charter' sounds like formulaic local government speak, as parents we do have a duty to try to bring up socially viable children. Raising our children is not merely a question of personal choice or style, but something that must be done in a way that meets our own satisfaction, as well as that of others. Conformity is not stultifying; it is necessary and liberating for us as a group. Civilising our children must become our rediscovered raison d'être. And those who find words like 'civilising' somewhat too Victorian for their taste might find it easier to embrace the notion of 'helping our lovely children to become even lovelier by developing their lovely, lovely social skills'.

Furthermore, we shouldn't shy away from the stigma that must be reconnected to having children who are 'deprived of social skills' i.e. spoilt. The return of accountability and shame for the parents of spoilt children will save our politicians, police, teachers and social workers hours of legislating and box-ticking, and may kick-start the self-regulating mechanism that has gone missing from our society and that creates what people call a 'community'.

If all of this sounds abstract and imperious, it needn't. For example, simply ensuring that our children don't eat in front of the television, but sit at a table together and with adults – preferably their own parents – can easily add twelve hours of parental/adult role-modelling (or civilising) time for our children every week. That's the equivalent of 104 full school days spent in an arena that allows them to absorb 'social skills'.

We must also absorb the emotional equation that we cannot

make up for our lack of time and attention by indulging our children, whether materially or in terms of our tolerance. It is the wrong currency for such a transaction and leads to behavioural and emotional inflation. During a recession, this should be a particularly timely equation to accept.

The extended parent

Parenting should be a far more seamless affair. Political commentators might refer to this idea, which existed for thousands of years cross-culturally, as the need for more joined-up parenting. Parenting, in the fullest sense of the word, follows our children out of the front door into the wider community. Unfortunately, however, the wider community is now – justifiably – reluctant and often frightened of fulfilling this role. The void must be reoccupied and there are very tangible steps that can be taken to this end.

Adults in many areas of our children's lives must be legally empowered to deal with them without the current fear that they may be prosecuted or punished for doing so. Dealing with our children may entail touching them, manhandling them and, if necessary, even hurting them in self-defence. There should be an absolute presumption that adults know better and are in the right, unless there are exceptional reasons. This is both a moral and legal imperative. Children of all ages must *know* this explicitly and implicitly – and, most importantly, *feel* this. Achieving such a reversal requires more than looking at the letter of the law: it is also a question of giving the police the latitude to use the law intelligently and expecting the prosecution service and the courts to interpret it in the same way.

Another significant arm of extended parenting is our children's teachers, and that too has been tied. Teachers are often not supported, but are instead challenged by parents when their children are chastised. The Schools Secretary has recently blamed parents for the misbehaviour of some pupils and urged schools not to let parental complaints about disciplinary sanctions undermine their authority. But teachers' authority has already been vastly weakened legally, professionally and culturally. Both teachers and pupils know that when push comes to shove, teachers can do neither. Given the sheer amount of time our children are in school, it is imperative that they do not spend this time learning that their extended parents have little authority in the face of a direct challenge. As with parenting and policing, there should be an absolute presumption that teachers know better and are in the right, unless it is shown otherwise. All elements of our teachers' authority – including manhandling, where necessary – have to be restored to the profession.

Interestingly, many people who would have previously baulked at the idea of a compulsory civic service for young people are beginning to take a different view. For example, the Labour MP Frank Field now believes the attitudes and behaviour of young people have reached a critical point. And although the idea of compulsory civic service 'cuts against the grain of autonomy and self-realisation – the holy writ of liberal societies – liberal societies cannot survive on liberalism alone. They need solidarity, service and authority too.' A mandatory national citizenship service programme would require young people aged between sixteen and twenty-five to spend at least six months working on projects helping children, sick or elderly people, the environment and international development. This would 'provide young people with structure, rites of passage, the opportunity to serve.'[1] But Field and others point to the importance for younger children to undergo collective forms of character-building through traditional routes of team sports and activities, like the Girl Guides, Brownies, cadets, the Boys' Brigade or orchestras. However, we know that children are more easily socialised when they are young, and so I believe we should encourage these activities very early on, even incorporating elements of civic service at infant and primary school.

In the child's best interests: revised edition

Children desperately need their fathers and their grandparents, especially at a point in our history when divorce, separation and fatherless households are at an all-time high. Fathers are indispensable and of paramount importance as figures of authority, being particularly good at understanding boundaries and policing them. If we want our children to be well adjusted and socially viable – and our society to be more civilised as a result – children need their fathers. And, most importantly, children need their fathers to have full licence to fulfil their roles and exert their authority.

Guaranteeing greater involvement of fathers and grandparents is absolutely crucial and requires changing laws and policies that don't reflect what is clearly best for children – the fact that both parents are equally vital to the wellbeing of their children. Without a cultural will presuming that there are ex-partners but no ex-fathers or ex-grandparents, reinforced by legal guarantees, our children won't have the benefit of their fathers acting as real fathers, nor the support and continuity that grandparents provide.

In a different way, mothers have also been kept from their children through a work and daycare ethos under the misguided banner of women's rights and a woman's choice. Child contact is far more important than either men's or women's rights. Parenthood transcends sexual politics and the child must be the prism through which our rights and choices are now viewed. A complete reversal of policy is needed in our children's best interests. Governments should not be providing incentives for mothers of young children to 'go back to work'. Rather, they should be enabling mothers to stay at home and provide their children with a superior upbringing to that provided by an institution.

Re-engineering

Much of what is suggested above involves changing or repealing laws. In response to this, I often hear excuses that usually boil down to: 'It's not as simple as that.' But I disagree. These changes *can* be made; and they could be made both simple and effective. In the best interests of our children, our politicians should make it happen – because that's their job. And where there's a will there's a way.

Politicians and the media have been very active in trying to change our attitudes and feelings about a wide variety of issues. I recently attended a meeting of minds in this very field, now called 'social marketing'. The industry magazine *PR Week* reported from it, saying that: 'Social marketing is expanding rapidly. According to the National Social Marketing Centre, the term refers to "the systematic application of marketing, alongside other concepts and techniques, to achieve specific behavioural goals for a social good".' Top industry and government representatives gathered (including the Director of PR and Communications at the Central Office of Information) to discuss the latest and most effective techniques to change our attitudes and behaviour around issues ranging from recreational drugs, to body fat, to recycling, to passive smoking, to 'the war on terror' and so on. The chief executive of one of Britain's top social marketing PR agencies explained, 'We did a campaign for the Commission for Racial Equality and the brief was to make people think positively about immigration. We did research and came up with the idea of using the British love of food. We asked celebrity chefs to come up with recipes of traditional English and well-loved foreign food to give people positive associations.' Other panellists shared their own experiences and tips.[2]

If we really care about our children, a master social marketing strategy is ready and waiting to return our distorted perceptions back to a timeless and universally observed state of betterment. Why not commission these social engineers to change their designs? Given that our social marketeers are so concerned about sweeping away the isms that bedevil certain groups of people, perhaps they should divert some of their resources away from the isms of skin tone and direct them, instead, to our greatest leveller – that which could restore authority and order to our children's lives: age and respect for the colour grey. That means recognising, in simple terms, that people who are older than you have greater authority, in the way that elders are positively revered in other cultures.

Whether it seems like an Eden project or a braver new world, making these changes would certainly be an improvement.

Through a combination of default, inexperience, circumstances, social fashion, and often sheer legal coercion, as parents, grandparents, teachers, lawmakers and policy-makers, we've retreated from parenting. We need to retrace our steps and find our way back. Fortunately I now sense a growing cultural will. And the path is clearly lit.

References

One: Little Emperors

1 Philippine Institute for Development Studies (PIDS). Forum 'Managing the Development Impact of International Migration'. Quote from Dr M. Cynthia Rose Bautista, 23 September 2008.
2 Professors John MacBeath and Maurice Galton, 'Pressure and Professionalism', from the University of Cambridge's Faculty of Education press release, 22 March 2008 (www.admin.cam.ac.uk/news/press/dpp/2008032201); and associated study, M. Galton, and J. MacBeath, 'Teachers Under Pressure', SAGE/National Union of Teachers, London, 2008.
3 UNICEF, 'Child Poverty in perspective: An Overview of Child Well-being in rich countries', UNICEF Innocenti Report Card 7, 2007.
4 The CAMHS Review, Jo Davidson, Bob Jezzard, 18 November 2008; www.dcsf.gov.uk/CAMHSreview.
5 General Teaching Council (GTC), 'Becoming a Teacher', July 2008.

Two: Friend or Führer?

1 Jerry M. Burger, 'Replicating Milgram: "Would People Still Obey Today?"', *American Psychologist*, volume 64, issue 1, pp. 1–11, January 2009.
2 S. Milgram, 'The Perils of Obedience', *Harper's Magazine*, pp. 62–77, December 1973; Milgram's article relates to his book, *Obedience to Authority: An Experimental View*, Pinter & Martin, London, 2005 (new edition).
3 Alexandra Shulman, (editor of *Vogue*), 'Help! I'm a Slave to My Son', column in *Daily Mail*, p. 50, 1 November 2008.
4 This is something I explored more fully in my book *Remotely Controlled*, Vermilion, London, 2007.

5   T. Benton, E. Cleaver, G. Featherstone, D. Kerr, J. Lopes and K. Whitby, Citizenship Education Longitudinal Study (CELS), Sixth Annual Report: 'Young People's Civic Participation In and Beyond School: Attitudes, Intentions and Influences' (DCSF Research Report 052), London, DCSF, 2008.

6   'Foot In Mouth', *Private Eye*, issue 1226, p. 3, 26 December 2008.

7   Adam Maroney, 'To Hug or Not to Hug', *CEC Today*, volume 4, number 5, November/December 1997.

8   UNICEF UK, 'Teaching about Children's Rights', 2008.

9   'What should be done to stop the spate of knife attacks?', *Croydon Today*, Friday 22 August 2008; www.thisiscroydontoday.co.uk/palacelatest/stop-spate-knife-attacks.

10 As reported by M. Phillips, 'The Dangerously Deluded Children's Tsar and the Truth about Knife Crime', *Daily Mail*, 25 May 2008.

11 Leslie Morrison Gutman, John Brown, Rodie Akerman, 'Nurturing Parenting Capability – The Early Years', Centre for Research on the Wider Benefits of Learning, Institute of Education, March 2009.

12 Patricio Cumsille, Nancy Darling, Brian Flaherty, M. Loreto Martínez, 'Heterogeneity and Change in the Patterning of Adolescents' Perceptions of the Legitimacy of Parental Authority: A Latent Transition Model', *Child Development*, volume 80, issue 2, pp. 313–17, 2009.

Three: Crime and Punishment

1   United Nations Convention on the Rights of the Child, Committee on the Rights of the Child, General Comment No. 8, CRC/C/GC/8, 2 March 2007.

2   W. James, *The Principles of Psychology*, volume 1, pp. 293–4, Dover, New York, 1950 (original work published 1890).

3   Z. Chen, K. D. Williams, J. Fitness and N. C. Newton, 'When Hurt Will Not Heal: Exploring the Capacity to Relive Social Pain', *Psychological Science*, volume 19, pp. 789–95, 2008.

4   Ara Norenzayan and Azim F. Shariff, 'The Origin and Evolution of Religious Prosociality', *Science*, volume 322, number 5898, pp. 58–623, October 2008, OI: 10.1126/science.1158757.

5   National Council of Resistance of Iran – Foreign Affairs Committee Iran, 'A prisoner hanged in Isfahan', Friday 31 October 2008.

6   David Cesarini, *et al*, 2009, 'Heritability of Cooperative Behavior in the Trust Game', Proceedings of the National Academy of Sciences, USA, 11 March 2008, 105(10): 3721–6, doi: 10.1073/pnas.0710069105.

7   Benjamin B. Lahey, Carol A. Van Hulle, Kate Keenan, Paul J. Rathouz, Brian M. D'Onofrio, Joseph Lee Rodgers, Irwin D. Waldman,

'Temperament and Parenting During the First Year of Life Predict Future Child Conduct Problems', *Journal of Abnormal Child Psychology*, volume 36, issue 8, pp. 1139–58, 2008.

Four: PC Parenting

1   Theodore Dwight, *The Father's Book*, G. and C. Merriam, Springfield, Mass., 1834.

2   Julia C. Nentwich, 'New Fathers and Mothers as Gender Troublemakers? Exploring Discursive Constructions of Heterosexual Parenthood and their Subversive Potential', *Feminism and Psychology*, volume 18, number 2, pp. 207–30, 2008.

3   Marianne G. Taylor, Marjorie Rhodes, Susan A. Gelman, 'Boys Will Be Boys; Cows Will Be Cows: Children's Essentialist Reasoning About Gender Categories and Animal Species, *Child Development*, volume 80, issue 2, pp. 461–81, 2009.

4   N. L. McElwain, A. G. Halberstadt and B. L. Volling, 'Mother- and Father-Reported Reactions to Children's Negative Emotions: Relations to Young Children's Emotional Understanding and Friendship Quality', *Child Development*, volume 78, issue 5, pp. 1407–25, 2007.

5   Kelly P. Cosgrove, Carolyn M. Mazure and Julie K. Staley, 'Evolving Knowledge of Sex Differences in Brain Structure, Function and Chemistry', *Biological Psychiatry*, volume 62, issue 8, pp. 847–55, 15 October 2007.

6   Marcella Bombardieri, 'Summers' Remarks on Women Draw Fire', *Boston Globe*, 17 January 2005; www.boston.com/news/local/articles/2005/01/17.

7   Steven Pinker, 'Boys Will Always be Boys', *Sunday Times*, News Review, p.3, 22 September 2002, interview, Steven Pinker by Margarette Driscoll.

8   Kyle D. Pruett, *Fatherneed: Why Father Care is as Essential as Mother Care for Your Child*, pp. 17–34, The Free Press, New York, 2000.

9   Nancy R. Gibbs, 'Where Are All the Fathers?', Time Archive, Saturday 16 June 2007.

10 Linda D. Ladd, 'What Fathers Contribute to Child Development', Texas Cooperative Extension, the Texas A&M University System, College Station, Texas, 2000.

11 Michelle Ball, 'Cognitive Processing During Sleep: the Role of Signal Significance and Participant Characteristics', p. 125, PhD thesis, Victoria University, School of Psychology Victoria University, Melbourne, Australia, 31 August 2007.

12 Sarah Evans, Nick Neave and Delia Wakelin, 'Relationships Between Vocal Characteristics and Body Size and Shape in Human Males: An

Evolutionary Explanation for a Deep Male Voice', *Biological Psychology*, volume 72, issue 2, pp. 160–63, May 2006.

13 Sarah Evans, Nick Neave, Delia Wakelin and Colin Hamilton, 'The Relationship Between Testosterone and Vocal Frequencies in Human Males', *Physiology and Behavior*, volume 93, issues 4–5, pp. 783–8, 18 March 2008.

14 Anne Karpf, *The Human Voice*, Bloomsbury Press, 2006.

15 British Voice Association, Gordon Stewart, August 2006; book review of *The Human Voice* by Anne Karpf, Bloomsbury Press, from 'Communicating Voice', British Voice Association; www.british-voice-association.com.

16 Cynthia L. Miller, Barbara A. Younger and Philip A. Morse, 'The Categorization of Male and Female Voices in Infancy', *Infant Behavior and Development*, volume 5, issues 2–4, pp. 143–59, 1982.

17 Dilraj S. Sokhi, Michael D. Hunter, Iain D. Wilkinson, and Peter W. R. Woodruff, 'Male and Female Voices Activate Distinct Regions in the Male Brain', *NeuroImage*, volume 27, issue 3, pp. 572–8, September 2005.

Five: Delegated Parenting

1 Aldous Huxley, *Brave New World* (1932); 2007 edition published by Vintage Classics, UK.

2 US Department of Labor: Bureau of Labor Statistics, Child Day Care Services, 2008; www.bls.gov.

3 Bethanne Kelly Patrick, 'Parenting by the Books – Lots of Them: The One Certainty in Childcare Titles These Days is Choice', *Publishers Weekly*, 2 December 2007.

4 Julia Dmitrieva, Laurence Steinberg and Jay Belsky, research report, 'Child-Care History, Classroom Composition, and Children's Functioning in Kindergarten', *Psychological Science*, volume 18, issue 12, pp. 1032–9, 2007.

5 Alexandra Frean, Education Editor, 'Nursery Children Arrive at School with Bad Attitude – and It Rubs Off', *The Times*, 5 January 2008.

6 Jay Belsky, *et al*, 'Are There Long-Term Effects of Early Child Care?', *Child Development*, volume 78, issue 2, pp. 681–701, 2007.

7 Sarah Womack, Social Affairs Correspondent, 'How Nurseries "Still Breed Aggression"', *Telegraph*, 19 April 2008.

8 Steve Doughty, 'Brown Advisor Calls for Tax Breaks for Stay-at-home Mums After Warning Over Nurseries', *Daily Mail*, 3 January 2008.

9 Jay Belsky, interview as reported in *LA Times* Archive for Thursday 26 April 2001, 'Researchers in Child-Care Study Clash Over Findings', by Jessica Garrison, 26 April 2001 in print edition A-1.

10 H. J. Vermeer and M. H. Van IJzendoorn, 'Children's Elevated Cortisol Levels at Daycare: A Review and Meta-analysis', *Early Childhood Research Quarterly*, volume 21, pp. 390–01, 2006.

11 G. I. Roisman, 'Early Family and Childcare Antecedents of Awakening Cortisol Levels in Adolescence', *Child Development*, volume 80, issue 3, pp. 907–20, 2009.

12 F. J. Zimmerman, *et al*, 'Associations Between Media Viewing and Language Development in Children Under Age 2 Years', *Journal of Pediatrics*, volume 151, issue 4, pp. 364–8, October 2007.

13 F. J. Zimmerman, *et al*, 'Television and DVD/Video Viewing in Children Younger Than 2 Years', *Archives of Pediatrics and Adolescent Medicine*, volume 161, issue 5, pp. 473–9, May 2007.

14 A. Poussaint, S. Linn, 'Say No to *Teletubbies*', www.familyeducation.com.

15 M. Krcmar, 'Learning Language From Television: Toddlers, Teletubbies and Attention', paper presented at the annual meeting of the International Communication Association, Sheraton New York, New York City, 10 October 2008; www.allacademic.com.

16 Marina Krcmar, Bernard Grela, Kirsten Lin, 'Can Toddlers Learn Vocabulary from Television? An Experimental Approach', *Media Psychology*, volume 10, number 1, pp. 41–63, 2007.

17 Barbara S. Kisilevsky, Sylvia M. J. Hains, Kang Lee, Xing Xie, Hefeng Huang, Hai Hui Ye, Ke Zhang, Zengping Wang, 'Effects of Experience on Fetal Voice Recognition', *Psychological Science*, volume 14, issue 3, pp. 220–24, 2003.

18 B. S. Kisilevsky, *et al*, 'Fetal Sensitivity to Properties of Maternal Speech and Language', *Infant Behavior and Development*, volume 32, issue 1, pp. 59–71, January 2009.

19 Huffman, *et al,* 'Cultured Monkeys: Social Learning Cast in Stones', *Current Directions in Psychological Science*, volume 17, issue 6, p. 410, 2008.

Six: Wait Till Your Mother Gets Home!

1 Office for National Statistics, ONS (2008), Social Trends, number 38.

2 González, L., 'The Effect of Benefits on Single Motherhood in Europe', *Labour Economics*, volume 14, issue 3, pp. 393–412, June 2007.

3 Matt O'Connor, founder of Fathers 4 Justice, quoted in report by Wesley Johnson: 'Fathers' Rights Duo Arrested at Gunpoint', *Scotsman*, 19 August 2007.

4 Gordon Brown, in a statement made to the press after the birth of his child, John, in 2003.

5 'Responsible Fatherhood Spotlight: Nonresident Fathers of Young Children', NRFC, US Department of Health and Human Services, 2007.

6 R. J. Quinlan, 'Father Absence, Parental Care, and Female Reproductive Development', *Evolution and Human Behavior*, volume 24, pp. 376–90, 2003.

7 Anthony F. Bogaert, 'Menarche and Father Absence in a National Probability Sample', *Journal of Biosocial Science*, volume 40, pp. 623–36, 2008.

8 B. J. Ellis, J. E. Bates, K. A. Dodge, D. M. Fergusson, J. L. Horwood, G. S. Pettit and L. Woodward, 'Does Father Absence Place Daughters at Special Risk for Early Sexual Activity and Teenage Pregnancy?', *Child Development*, volume 74, pp. 801–21, 2003.

9 Kevin Finn, Neil Johannsen and Bonny Specker, 'Factors Associated with Physical Activity in Preschool Children', *Journal of Pediatrics*, volume 140, pp. 81–5, January 2002.

10 Sandra Hofferth and Kermit G. Anderson, 'Biological and Stepfather Investment in Children', PSC research report number 01–484, PSC Publications Population Studies Center, University of Michigan, 8 March 2001.

11 'One Parent Families', One Parent Families|Gingerbread mission statement, www.oneparentfamilies.org.uk.

12 P. R. Amato, J. Cheadle, 'The Long Reach of Divorce: Divorce and Child Well-being Across Three Generations', *Journal of Marriage and Family*, volume 67, issue 1, pp. 191–206, February 2005.

13 Alison Blackwell and Fiona Dawe, 'Non-Resident Parental Contact', based on data from the National Statistics Omnibus Survey for the Department for Constitutional Affairs, October 2003; Social and Vital Statistics Division, Office for National Statistics.

14 Data from Age Concern and the Grandparents' Association, reported by Rhodri Clark, *Western Mail*, 19 March 2008 by Rhodri Clark.

15 Jenny Johnston and Rachel Halliwell, 'Jailed for Waving at My Daughter', *Daily Mail*, pp. 28–9, 25 June 2007; Mark Harris, *Family Court Hell*, Pen Press Publishers Ltd, UK, 2007.

16 Rosemary Bennett, 'Vengeful Mothers Leave Good Fathers Powerless to See Child, Says Judge', *The Times*, 1 May 2008.

17 Professor M. Rosario Cortés Arboleda, Professor José Cantón Duarte and Professor M. Dolores Justicia Díaz, 'One Out of Four Children Involved in a Divorce Undergoes Parental Alienation Syndrome', press release, Department of Evolutionary and Educational Psychology of the University of Granada, 22 January 2008.

18 R. A. Gardner, 'The Three Levels of Parental Alienation Syndrome Alienators', *American Journal of Forensic Psychiatry*, volume 25, issue 41, 2004.

19 Dr L. F. Lowenstein, 'Parental Alienation and the Judiciary', *Medico-Legal Journal*, volume 67, part 3, pp. 121–3, 1999.

20 Augustine J. Kposowa, 'Marital Status and Suicide in the National Longitudinal Mortality Study', *Journal of Epidemiology and Community Health*, volume 54, pp. 254–261, April 2000.

21 Sharon Hoogland, Randall Pieterse, 'Suicide in Australia: A Dying Shame', published by Wesley Mission, Sydney, 'LifeForce', Suicide Prevention Week, 6–10 November 2000; www.wesleymission.org.au/publications.

22 Ashley Barnett-White, 'In Memory of Darrin White', www.equalparenting-bc.ca/testimonials/white_ashlee and www.foxnews.com/story.

23 www.fathercare.org.

24 Linda Nielsen, 'Shared Parenting: Facts and Fiction', Research Brochure, American Coalition for Fathers and Children, 2008, http://acfc.convio.net.

25 Linda Nielsen Home Page, 2009, http://www.wfu.edu/~nielsen/resume.htm.

26 American Coalition for Fathers and Children, http://acfc.convio.net.

27 Marsha Kline Pruett, 'Fathers Parent Differently than Mothers: Implications for Children and Families Before, During or After Divorce', presentation to the Association of Family and Conciliation Courts, in collaboration with University of Baltimore School of Law, University of Baltimore, 10–11 December 2008.

Seven: The Restructured Unit

1 E Home Fellowship, 'Blended Family Problems', www.way2hope.org.

Eight: The Three-parent Family

1 'What Children Watch: an Analysis of Children's Programming Provision', Broadcasting Standards Commission and the Independent Television Commission, June 2003.

2 A. Szabo, Katey L. Hopkinson, 'Negative Psychological Effects of Watching the News in the Television: Relaxation or Another Intervention May Be Needed to Buffer Them!', *International Journal of Behavioral Medicine*, volume 14, issue 2, pp. 57–62, 2007.

3 BMRB International (British Market Research Bureaux), 'Increasing Screen Time is Leading to Inactivity of 11–15s', Youth TGI Study, 2004.

4 Joel Schwarz, 'Baby DVDs, videos may hinder, not help, infants' language development' in news release, University of Washington, 7 August 2007, on study carried out by Frederick J. Zimmerman.

5 R. Winston, 'The Damning Proof that TV Does Corrupt Our Young',

editorial accompanying BBC documentary series *Child of Our Time*, written for *Daily Mail*, p. 12, 9 January 2004.

6 ChildWise Monitor, Trends Report, 2008.

7 F. J. Zimmerman, *et al*, 'Television and DVD/Video Viewing in Children Younger Than Two Years', *Archive of Pediatrics and Adolescent Medicine*, volume 161, issue 5, pp. 473–9, May 2007.

8 Children's Society, 'The Good Childhood Inquiry', published UK, 25 February 2008.

9 Ezekiel J. Emanuel, Cary P. Gross, Helen M. Huang, Marcella Nunez-Smith and Elizabeth Wolf, 'Media and Child and Adolescent Health: A Systematic Review', *Common Sense Media*, volume 3, issue 8, 2008.

10 Dimitri A. Christakis, 'The Effects of Infant Media Usage: What Do We Know and What Should We Learn?' *Acta Paediatrica*, volume 98, issue 1, pp. 8–16, 2009.

11 Jessica Nicoll, BA, and Kevin M. Kieffer, PhD, 'Violence in Video Games: A Review of the Empirical Research', presentation at Session 2185, 113th Annual Convention of the American Psychological Association in Washington, DC, 19 August 2005.

12 L. Twist, I. Schagen, *et al*, 'Readers and Reading: The National Report for England 2006' (PIRLS: Progress in International Reading Literacy Study), Slough, 2007.

13 R. Kawashima, *et al*, reported in *World Neurology*, volume 3, issue 3, 16 September 2001.

14 G. Gerbner, 'Learning Productive Aging as a Social Role: The Lessons of Television' in S. A. Bass, F. G. Caro, Y. P. Chen, (eds), *Achieving a Productive Aging Society*, Greenwood Publishing Group, Westport, 1993.

15 Sigman, *Remotely Controlled*, Vermilion, London, 2007.

16 Gary Small, *et al*, 'Your Brain on Google: Patterns of Cerebral Activation During Internet Searching', *American Journal of Geriatric Psychiatry*, volume 17, issue 2, February 2009.

17 A. Sigman, 'Well Connected? The Biological Implications of "Social Networking"', *Biologist*, volume 56, issue 1, pp. 14–20, 2009.

18 J. Bradshaw, *et al*, 'An Index of Child Well-being in the European Union Social Indicators Research', volume 80, number 1, pp. 133–77(45), January 2007.

19 P. Spungin, National Family Mealtime Survey, 2004, Raisingkids.co.uk.

20 Speech by Dr John Dunford, General Secretary, at the Association of School and College Leaders' annual conference, Brighton, 7 March 2008.

21 Giacomo Rizzolatti, 'How Mirror Neurons Help Us Understand Insights of Others and Are Impaired in Autism', *Neurology Today*,

volume 8, issue 12, pp. 20–21, 19 June 2008; and presidential lecture by Giacomo Rizzolatti, 'The Mirror Neuron System', at the American Academy of Neurology 60th annual meeting, Chicago, 11 April 2008.

22 M. A. Umiltà, L. Escola, I. Intskirveli, F. Grammont, M. Rochat, F. Caruana, A. Jezzini, V. Gallese and G. Rizzolatti, 'When Pliers Become Fingers in the Monkey Motor System', Proceedings of the National Academy of Sciences, PNAS, volume 105, number 6, pp. 2209–13, 12 February 2008.

23 Jennifer H. Pfeifer, et al, 'Mirroring Others' Emotions Relates to Empathy and Interpersonal Competence in Children', NeuroImage, volume 39, issue 4, pp. 2076–85, February 2008.

24 Yuki, et al, 'Are the Windows to the Soul the Same in the East and West? Cultural Differences in Using the Eyes and Mouth as Cues to Recognize Emotions in Japan and the United States', Journal of Experimental Social Psychology, volume 43, issue 2, pp. 303–11, 2007.

25 A. Abu-Akel, 'The Psychological and Social Dynamics of Topic Performance in Family Dinnertime Conversation', Journal of Pragmatics, volume 34, number 12, pp. 1787–1806, 2002.

26 S. S. Luthar, S. J. Latendresse, 'Children of the Affluent. Challenges to Well-Being', Current Directions in Psychological Science, volume 14, issue 1, pp. 49–53, 2005.

27 Tania Murray Li, 'Working Separately But Eating Together: Personhood, Property, and Power in Conjugal Relations', American Ethnologist, volume 25, issue 4, pp. 675–94, 1998.

28 CASA (2008), the National Center on Addiction and Substance Abuse at Columbia University, www.casafamilyday.org.

29 CASA (2005), the National Center on Addiction and Substance Abuse at Columbia University, 'The Importance of Family Dinners. National Center on Addiction and Substance Abuse at Columbia', statements reported by Fox News – Health: 'Family Meals Help Teens Avoid Smoking, Alcohol, Drugs', www.foxnews.com/story.

30 National Family Month (2006), 'National family month 2006 to provide opportunities to tackle top health, safety and social issues facing families today', 8 May, http://www.nationalfamilymonth.net.

31 D. Neumark-Sztainer, et al, 'Family Meals and Disordered Eating in Adolescents: Longitudinal Findings From Project EAT', Archive of Pediatrics and Adolescent Medicine, volume 162, issue 1, pp. 17–22, 2008.

32 Larson, et al, 'Family Meals During Adolescence Are Associated with Higher Diet Quality and Healthful Meal Patterns During Young Adulthood', Journal of the American Dietetic Association, volume 107, issue 9, pp. 1502–10, 2007.

33 T. V. Cooper, et al, 'An assessment of obese and non-obese girls'

metabolic rate during television viewing, reading, and resting', *Eating Behaviors*, volume 7, issue 2, pp. 105–14, 2006.

34 N. Stroebele, J. M. de Castro, 'Television Viewing is Associated with an Increase in Meal Frequency in Humans', *Appetite*, volume 42, issue 1, pp. 111–13, February 2003.

35 L. H. Epstein, *et al*, 'Allocation of Attentional Resources During Habituation to Food Cues', *Psychophysiology*, volume 34, issue 1, pp. 59–64, 1997.

36 J. L. Temple, A. M. Giacomelli, K. M. Kent, J. N. Roemmich, L.H. Epstein, 'Television Watching Increases Motivated Responding and Energy Intake in Children', *American Journal of Clinical Nutrition*, volume 85, issue 2, pp. 355–61, 2007.

37 S. Gable, 'Television Watching and Frequency of Family Meals Are Predictive of Overweight Onset and Persistence in a National Sample of School-Aged Children', *Journal of the American Dietetic Association*, volume 107, issue 1, pp. 53–61, January 2007.

38 UCSD, '"Love Hormone" Promotes Bonding', news release from University of California, San Diego (UCSD) School of Medicine, 7 February 2008.

39 P. J. Zak, A. A. Stanton, S. Ahmadi, 'Oxytocin Increases Generosity in Humans', 2007, Public Library of Science PLoS ONE 2(11): e1128, doi:10.1371/journal.pone.0001128

40 Comments by first author of study, Mary Helen Immordino-Yang, reported from news press release University of Southern California, 13 April 2009.

41 Mary Helen Immordino-Yang, Andrea McColl, Hanna Damasio and Antonio Damasio, 'Neural Correlates of Admiration and Compassion', Proceedings of the National Academy of Sciences, 2009; www.pnas.org.

42 ChildWise Monitor, 2009.

Nine: Spoilt for Choice

1 Sheena S. Iyengar, Mark R. Lepper, 'When Choice is Demotivating: Can One Desire Too Much of a Good Thing?', *Journal of Personality and Social Psychology*, volume 79, number 6, pp. 995–1006, December 2006; www.columbia.edu.

2 A. de Tocqueville, *Democracy in America*, Harper & Row, New York, 1969.

3 Report on SANEP (South African Nutrition Experts Panel) exercise and nutrition study, 'Nation Needs to Move on Diet and Exercise: A New Research Study Lifts the Lid on Kids, Nutrition and Exercise', www.clover.co.za/live/content, 2007.

4 Huxley, op. cit. reference 1, Chapter Five.

5 O. R. W. Pergams, and P. A. Zaradic, 'Evidence for a fundamental and pervasive shift away from nature-based recreation', Proceedings of the National Academy of Sciences, 105:7, pp. 2295–300, 2008.

6 F. E. Kuo, A. F. Taylor, 'A Potential Natural Treatment for Attention-Deficit/hyperactivity Disorder: Evidence from a National Study', American Journal of Public Health, volume 94, issue 9, pp. 1580–86, 2004.

7 A. F. Taylor and F. E. Kuo, 'Children with Attention Deficits Concentrate Better After Walk in the Park', Journal of Attention Disorders, volume 12, issue 5, pp. 402–9, March 2009.

8 A. F. Taylor, F. E. Kuo, W. C. Sullivan, 'Views of Nature and Self Discipline: Evidence from Inner-City Children', Journal of Environmental Psychology, volume 21, 2001.

9 P. Groenewegen, et al, 'Vitamin G: Effects of Green Space on Health, Wellbeing, and Social Safety BMC Public Health', volume 6, p. 149, 2006.

10 T. M. Waliczek, et al, 'Using a Web-based Survey to Research the Benefits of Children Gardening', Horticultural Technology, volume 10, pp. 71–6, 2000.

Ten: Bigging Them Up

1 R. Baumeister, 'The Lowdown on High Self-Esteem', Los Angeles Times, 25 January 2005.

2 M. H. Kernis, C. E. Lakey, and W. L. Heppner, 'Secure Versus Fragile High Self-esteem as a Predictor of Verbal Defensiveness: Converging Findings Across Three Different Markers', Journal of Personality, volume 76, pp. 1–36, 2008; and press release from University of Georgia, 'High Self-esteem is Not Always What It's Cracked Up to Be', 28 April 2008.

Eleven: The Devil's Buttermilk

1 K. L. Medina, et al, 'Prefrontal Cortex Volumes in Adolescents with Alcohol Use Disorders: Unique Gender Effects', Alcoholism: Clinical and Experimental Research, volume 32, issue 3, pp. 386–94, March 2008.

2 M. D. De Bellis, et al, 'Diffusion Tensor Measures of the Corpus Callosum in Adolescents with Adolescent Onset Alcohol Use Disorders', Alcoholism: Clinical and Experimental Research, volume 32, issue 3, pp. 395–404, March 2008.

3 The Alcohol Research Consortium, www.gla.ac.uk/schools/dental/researchactivities/biotechnologyandcraniofacial/researchactivities/alcoholrelatedfacialinjuries.

4   J. Bradshaw, P. Hoelscher, and D. Richardson, 'Comparing Child Well-being in OECD Countries: Concepts and Methods', Innocenti Working Paper (IWP 2006-03), UNICEF, Florence, December 2006.

5   C. Currie, *et al* (eds), 'Inequalities in Young People's Health: HBSC international report from the 2005/2006 Survey', WHO Regional Office for Europe, Copenhagen, 2008 (Health Policy for Children and Adolescents, number 5).

6   ESPAD Report, 'The 2007 European School Survey Project on Alcohol and Other Drugs', released 26 March 2009; British contributing author Martin Plant added further comment in article, 'UK teenagers among heaviest drinkers in EU', *Guardian*, 27 March 2009.

7   Professor Ian Gilmore, president of the Royal College of Physicians, in a statement, 24 December 2006.

8   C. A. Goodall, A. F. Ayoub, A. Crawford, I. Smith, A. Bowman, D. Koppel, G. Gilchrist, 'Nurse-delivered Brief Interventions for Hazardous Drinkers with Alcohol-related Facial Trauma: A Prospective Randomised Controlled Trial', *British Journal of Oral Maxillofacial Surgery*, volume 46, issue 2, pp. 89–176, 2008.

9   D. Nutt, L. A. King, W. Saulsbury and C. Blakemore, 'Development of a Rational Scale to Assess the Harm of Drugs of Potential Misuse', *Lancet*, volume 369, pp. 1047–53, 2007.

10 Hywel Hughes, Rachael Peters, Gareth Davies, Keith Griffiths, 'A Study of Patients Presenting to an Emergency Department Having Had a "Spiked Drink"', *Emergency Medicine Journal*, volume 24, pp. 89–91, 2007.

11 S. L. Greene, *et al*, 'What's Being Used to Spike Your Drink? Alleged Spiked Drink Cases in Inner City London', *Postgraduate Medical Journal*, volume 83, pp. 754–8, 2007.

12 'Pupils aged 12 "were drunk after school taught them wine tasting"', reported in the *Daily Mail*, p. 9, 21 March 2009.

13 Department for Children, Schools and Families, 'Use of Alcohol among Children and Young People', published 30 October 2008, Report Publication Code: DCSF-RW043.

14 Directorate-General for Health and Consumer Protection, European Commission, Fact Sheet, 'Alcohol-Related Harm in Europe', 2006.

15 Alcohol Concern statement, 'Call to stop children's drinking', reported by BBC News 27 April 2007; http://news.bbc.co.uk/go/pr/fr/-/1/hi/uk/6596515.stm.

16 S. Gupta, J. Warner, 'Alcohol-related Dementia: A 21st-century Silent Epidemic?' *British Journal of Psychiatry*, volume 193, pp. 351–3, 2008.

17 Deborah A. Dawson, Risë B. Goldstein, S. Patricia Chou, W. June Ruan, Bridget F. Grant, 'Age at First Drink and the First Incidence of

Adult-Onset DSM-IV Alcohol Use Disorders', *Alcoholism: Clinical and Experimental Research*, volume 32, issue 12, pp. 2149–60, 2008.

18 'Children under 15 should not drink any alcohol, says chief medical officer', guardian.co.uk, Thursday 29 January, 2009; www.guardian.co.uk/society/2009/jan/29/alcohol-children-health.

19 Adam Edwards, 'Drinks are in the House: Has New Labour watered down Westminster's convivial drinking habits, asks Adam Edwards', telegraph.co.uk, 7 November 2002.

20 Speech by the Right Honourable Alan Johnson MP, Secretary of State for Health, 'Nanny State, Nudge State or No State?' at the Royal Society of Arts, 19 March 2009.

Twelve: Dethroning the Emperors

1 Frank Field, James Crabtree, 'Citizenship First: The Case for Compulsory Civic Service', *Prospect*, issue 156, March 2009.

2 Alex Black, 'For the greater good', *PR Week* UK, 31 January 2008.

Index